*Leonardo Faccio*

# MESSI

Leonardo Faccio was born in Buenos Aires in 1971. He has spent the last ten years living in Barcelona, where he writes for various publications, including *El Periódico* and *Etiqueta Negra*, and received an honorable mention from the Gabriel García Márquez Iberoamerican Foundation for New Journalism. He was not a fan of soccer until he first learned of Lionel Messi.

# MESSI

# MESSI

*A Biography*

LEONARDO FACCIO

*Translated from the Spanish by Cecilia Molinari*

**ANCHOR SPORTS**
*Anchor Books*
*A Division of Random House, Inc. – New York*

AN ANCHOR SPORTS ORIGINAL, SEPTEMBER 2012

*English translation copyright © 2012 by Anchor Books,*
*a division of Random House, Inc.*

The Cataloging-in-Publication Data for *Messi* is available at the
Library of Congress.

ISBN: 978-0-345-80269-9

*Book design by Claudia Martinez*
*Cover design by Katya Mezhibovskaya*
*Cover photograph © Matthew Ashton / AMA / Corbis*

www.anchorbooks.com

Printed in the United States of America
12 14 16 18 20 19 17 15 13 11

*To my father, Italo Faccio*

*And to Monica Porta Dominguez*

*Per obrir totes les portes.*
(For opening all doors.)

# CONTENTS

------------------------

# PART ONE

---------------------------

## 2009

# I

Lionel Messi has just returned from a Disney World vacation, dragging his flip-flops with that lack of glamour so typical of resting athletes. He could have continued his time off in Argentina or in any Caribbean country, but he opted to return to Barcelona early: Messi wants to train. Sometimes vacations bore him. He's sitting on a chair in a deserted soccer field in the Ciutat Esportiva, FC Barcelona's sports center, which operates in a valley secluded from the residential area of the city, a bright cement-and-glass lab where coaches turn talented soccer players into precision machines. Messi is a player with no instruction manual, and Ciutat Esportiva is his incubator. He has agreed to give a fifteen-minute interview this afternoon, and he looks happy. After touring with his club through the United States, he spent some time at Disney World with his parents, siblings, uncles, cousins, nephews, and girlfriend. Disney had seen Messi as the perfect person to promote its world of illusions, and Messi's entire family was given access to all the rides as long as he allowed himself to be filmed in the gardens within this cartoon empire. Today, on YouTube, we can see a smiling Messi, performing miracles with a soccer ball in front of the fantastical architecture of the park.

"We had an amazing time," says Messi with enthusiasm. "It finally happened."

"What did you like most at Disney World?"

"The water rides, the parks, the attractions. Everything. Above all, I went for my nieces and nephews, my cousins, and my sister. But when I was a kid, I had always wanted to go."

"Was it like a dream?"

"Yes, I think so, right? At least for kids fifteen and under, but also if you're a little older."

As we sit face-to-face at Ciutat Esportiva, Messi ponders each of his words before letting them out, as if every so often he needs to confirm that we have understood him, as if he were requesting permission to speak. As a child he suffered from a type of dwarfism, a growth hormone disorder, and since then, his short height has only magnified his soccer stature. Up close, Messi has that contradictory appearance of child gymnasts: legs with bulging muscles below, yet shy, inquisitive eyes above. He's a warrior with a child's gaze.

However, at times, it inevitably feels as if one has come to interview Superman and is instead met by one of Disney's vulnerable and absentminded heroes.

"Who is your favorite Disney character?"

"None in particular, because as a kid I didn't really watch many cartoons." He smiles. "And then I came here to play soccer."

When Messi says the word *fútbol*, his smile disappears and he becomes as serious as if he were about to take a penalty kick. It's that cautious look we are so used to seeing on TV. Messi usually doesn't smile while he plays. The soccer business is too serious: Only twenty-five countries in the world produce a larger GDP than the soccer industry. It is the world's most popular sport, and Messi is the star of the show. Months after his Disney World trip, he'd achieve more than any other player his age ever has. He would go on to win six consecutive titles with FC Barcelona, becoming the European league's top scorer; he'd be chosen as the best soccer player in the world; he'd establish himself as the youngest player to score one hundred goals in his club's storied history; and he'd become the sport's highest-paid star, with an annual contract worth 10.5 million euros—ten times what Diego Maradona earned while playing at Barça. Messi would fly to Zurich to accept Europe's best soccer player award, the Ballon d'Or, in a tailor-made Italian suit. But this afternoon, his bangs are parted to the side, he has a crooked smile, and he's wearing Barça's fluorescent green jersey over a pair of training shorts. He's one of the main hosts in soccer's wheel of fortune, yet today he looks like an unkempt boy who's come to see the show.

After juggling a soccer ball at Disney World, Messi still had a few weeks of vacation left and decided to go back to the city where he was born. Rosario is located north of Buenos Aires, in Santa Fe Province. It's the third-largest city in Argentina and Che Guevara's birthplace. The newest soccer prodigy spent his time with childhood friends and at his parents' home in the Las Heras neighborhood. However, a week before his vacation came to an end, he packed his bags and returned to Barcelona, where his dog, a boxer named Facha, always welcomes him home. Messi lives alone with this dog; his mother, father, and sister visit him during certain times of the year. The press wondered why a superstar soccer player would cut his vacation time, which is usually so scarce, short. Messi told them he returned early to train and stay in good shape. At the time, he was playing the qualifying rounds for the South Africa World Cup with Argentina's national soccer team. Maradona was his head coach, and Messi knew it could be his first World Cup in the starting lineup as number 10. He wanted to return to Barcelona to continue the show; plus he was bored in Rosario.

"When I go to Rosario, I love it. I have my home, my people, everything. But it tires me because I don't do anything," he says with a shrug. "I was just lounging around all day and that also gets boring."

"Don't you watch TV?"

"I started to watch *Lost* and *Prison Break*, but they tired me out."

"Why did you stop watching them?"

"Because something new was always going on, a new story line, and then someone else would tell me about it."

Messi gets bored with *Lost*.

Messi is left-handed.

At first glance, it seems as though he has a fetish with his right leg: He strokes it as if he occasionally has to soothe it. Later, one notices that the object of his affection is not his hyperactive leg but rather the BlackBerry in his pocket. Outstanding soccer players have habits that draw them closer to the rest of us mere mortals, which seems to normalize their brilliance. It was said that Johan Cruyff smoked in the locker room minutes before going out on the field. Maradona trained with untied shoelaces and said that if not for a set regulation, he would have played official games the same way. Romário went dancing at night and said that the samba helped him become the top scorer in the league. Most successful soccer players constantly purchase things that flaunt their present affluence rather than secure their future. New sports cars, eye-catching clothes, flamboyant watches. However, while Ronaldinho rented his house in Castelldefels, Messi bought his home just three blocks away: a two-story building located on a hilltop overlooking the Mediterranean. Far from the superstar caricature with the gold Rolex, huge Gucci sunglasses, and blond bombshell on his arm, Messi's the type who gets bored with new TV shows, although he does appreciate fashionable colognes. His family knows that a gift-wrapped fragrance will get a smile out of him.

"So what's a normal day like for you after practice?" I ask.

"I like to take a siesta. And at night, I don't know . . . I go have dinner at my brother's."

By accepting this interview, Messi has deprived himself of a ritual he has maintained since his childhood. Every day, after soccer practice at the club, he eats and goes to sleep, awakening two to three hours later. (Olympic swimming champion Michael Phelps's coach once declared that Phelps took a three-hour siesta daily to recuperate from training.) Messi normally does not interrupt his routine. The siesta, to him, is like a ceremony whose purpose has changed with time. He always follows the same customs. He doesn't use the queen-size bed he has in his room; he flops onto his living-room sofa, fully clothed. He doesn't care if someone washes the dishes in the kitchen or slams a door shut while he sleeps. As a child, this resting period, in addition to the medication, helped with his cell regeneration. Messi slept to grow. Nowadays, he no longer needs to grow; he explains he has other reasons that justify these siestas. Similar to Phelps and other soccer players, he takes a siesta to recover his strength, but above all, he naps because he doesn't feel like doing anything else after leaving the soccer ball behind. The numerous forms of entertainment that he could afford sooner or later just tire him. Taking a vacation is another way of buying a distraction, and it also bores him. The siesta seems to be his antidote. No one gets bored while sleeping.

There's a certain mystery surrounding geniuses whom we're drawn to, which is normal. Fans will go to great lengths to touch their idols. It's a way of proving they are real. On the other hand, reporters ask them questions to find out if their private world is similar to us mortals'.

"Is it true that you're addicted to video games?" a reporter from the newspaper *El Periódico de Catalunya* once asked.

"I used to be into them. I don't play as much now."

"Do you watch soccer on TV?" inquired a journalist from the newspaper *El País*.

"No, I don't watch soccer. I'm not one to watch."

Hundreds of journalists have yearned to interview Messi one-on-one.

One even risked his life trying to do so.

Messi didn't seem to notice. One night, after a King's Cup match, a man facing a death threat was waiting for him in the tunnels that lead to the FC Barcelona locker rooms. It was writer Roberto Saviano. He had sought him out to meet him, knowing full well that he could also get killed there. Since he exposed the Naples mafia in his book *Gomorrah*, his whereabouts have been unknown, and he lives and breathes with a team of ten bodyguards by his side 24/7. That night they found him a seat out of sniper's range. He wanted to meet Messi in person, shake his hand, get his autograph, and ask him a few questions. He was hoping to talk to him on his own, but his bodyguards refused to leave his side, saying they were following orders. They also were dying to see the soccer player who dreamed of going to Disney World.

One waits fifteen months to get fifteen minutes with him.

To Saviano, who was risking his life to meet him, Messi said he would feel right at home in Naples.

He gave him about twenty words.

That's it.

Today, in Ciutat Esportiva, after telling me about his Disney vacation, Messi raises his eyebrows like a silent movie actor expecting more questions. He's like a smiling mime with constantly changing expressions. The electricity discharged from his body on soccer fields makes him comparable to PlayStation video game characters. Lionel Messi requires metaphors that are less electric and more surreal. The guy who entertains millions of us finds nothing better to do with his afternoons than lie down and sleep.

# 2

Messi talks mostly soccer with strangers. One of the exceptions is when he orders food for delivery. This day, Messi's butcher parks his delivery truck in front of his most famous client's house and, with a tourist guide's gesture, shows me the security cameras set atop the building's façade. It's three p.m. and Messi is probably sleeping. The street is quiet, no one climbing the curvy Castelldefels hill to contemplate the Mediterranean. When Messi wants to barbecue, he calls the butcher and he delivers the order of steaks, offal, and chorizos. The butcher, an Argentine nicknamed "El Gallego" by his friends, has offered to be my guide. La Pampa, the restaurant where he works, serves barbecue and sells and delivers Argentine beef. Messi's house is at the top of a hill, at the end of a narrow road surrounded by pine trees. There's no public transportation around here. It's an ideal place for silence.

Talking with Messi is a privilege enjoyed by people like

his coach, his dad, and his butcher. Although sometimes his coach is not as lucky: Maradona, who trained him on Argentina's national team, said that getting Messi to answer his phone was harder than interviewing God. When playing detective, informants are divided into those who boast about knowing this star in person and those who remember meeting him before fame removed them from his world.

Mónica Dómina was his teacher at the elementary school in Las Heras. One night, we had a phone conversation revolving around the years when Messi occupied the first desk in her classroom.

"Did you teach him how to read and write?"

"Yes, but he didn't like school at all. He did it as an obligation."

Dómina's voice has a teacher's maternal tone and the solemnity of someone who's reading a will.

"He was very shy," she tells me. "I had major issues communicating with him."

"And what did you do to encourage him to speak up?"

"He had a friend who sat behind him and told me everything he wanted to say."

"Did she act like his interpreter?"

"Yes. She even bought his afternoon snacks. She was like a mother with a little boy. And he let her manage it all for him."

At the age when all children are bursting with questions, Leo Messi communicated with his teacher through a six-year-old spokesperson. Nowadays, as with all authentic geniuses, no teachers are acknowledged. "It's as if Messi still does not treat himself with that level of respect," says

Jorge Valdano. "To reach those levels of celebrity and not get confused is impossible, unless one is highly gifted or autistic." Lionel Messi is accused of living in a bubble.

"Did he need a child psychologist?"

"I recommended his mom take him to a psychologist," insists the teacher. "He had to leave his shyness behind and reinforce his self-esteem. His was very low."

Today, Messi's butcher is in very high spirits. The restaurant where he works has included its star client's name in its marketing plan. The maître d' offers fans a guided tour through a rustic scene: photos of horses hanging on the walls, waiters dressed as gauchos, and a sign with a bull's head at the entrance. La Pampa is a highway restaurant with a wine list, only a five-minute drive from Messi's home. At noon on Sundays, someone always arrives asking if that's where the idol comes to eat his favorite food.

"Is it true that what he most asks for is *milanesa a la napolitana*?"

"No, at least not here," notes the maître d'. "Messi always eats the same thing: short ribs."

That's what his dilemma outside the field is all about: choosing between short ribs or *milanesa a la napolitana* (Argentina's veal Parmesan). A psychiatrist would have serious difficulties trying to wring out more intimate details from him on a divan. Messi prefers sofas for siestas.

"So did Messi end up going to a psychologist?" I ask the teacher.

"I don't remember," she says regretfully. "What I do remember is that his mom always brought the trophies he won at soccer to class. But he would die of embarrassment."

"Did you have other students as shy as him?"

"No. He was different. Everyone wanted to play with him."

Dómina quickly goes on. She wants to say more.

"He was a silent leader," she says, as if she were clenching the phone. "He led by action, not words. I see he's still the same now."

"What image do you remember him by?"

"I see him as small and restless, with that smile that made you think he is hiding something or up to something."

"Have you seen him again since he graduated your class?"

"Never."

The teacher goes quiet.

Yet somehow, Messi still helps the school: He's donated desks, school supplies, and computers.

Nowadays, he observes the world through his large windows overlooking the Mediterranean. It's a still landscape that condemns the security cameras to boredom. They are there in case something happens, but most of the time nothing happens. If the butcher knows of any secrets, he won't tell me. He'll barely throw me a bone, like those thrown at a dog that will return it to its owner. Before hopping on the delivery truck to come here, the maître d' stopped me at table twelve in the restaurant to share a piece of news. One night, Messi arrived with a girl in his Audi Q7, the car the club gives to all the players. They ordered short ribs and chorizo, and dulce de leche ice cream for dessert. It was a candlelit dinner. Messi introduced the woman as his girlfriend.

# 3

Leo Messi is getting annoyed by all my questions regarding his vacation. He strokes his leg, where he keeps his phone, and his gaze hovers beyond the trees that surround Ciutat Esportiva. This afternoon, his eyes dart back and forth as if following a ball in a Ping-Pong game. Then, I remind him of a newspaper article and suddenly the headline returns him to this orbit. It's about his girlfriend. It was a carnival day in Sitges, a town southwest of Barcelona with a Caribbean feel that plays host to gay vacationers and a fantastic film festival. The sun imitated a spring day. In the photograph, Messi, who lives a few miles away, walked arm in arm with a girl whose height slightly passed his shoulders. The photo announced a name: Antonella Roccuzzo. A petite girl with a stunning last name.

"What about the girlfriend thing?" I ask him. "Is it true?"

"Yes, we've known each other since we were kids," he

says, as if opening a candy wrapper. "She's my best friend's cousin."

Messi has friends.

His best friend is Lucas Scaglia.

*My Best Friend's Cousin* sounds like an Italian movie title. A B movie.

One day, Scaglia explains it over the phone.

In Newell's Old Boys little league soccer club in Rosario, the boys were kamikazes. Scaglia was kamikaze number 5. Messi was a great but shy scorer. When they met, they were just starting elementary school. Sometimes, he would sleep over at Scaglia's.

Messi diminishes the melodrama.

"So, did you see the cousin at his house?" I ask him at Ciutat Esportiva.

He leans in, as if he is about to divulge secret tips on how to score more points in a video game, but instead says:

"We both used to play together as kids. And it ended up as a relationship."

The Messi family originated from Recanati, the poet Giacomo Leopardi's city. Within the big community of immigrants in Rosario, the Italians are the largest group. His mother is Celia Cuccittini. His cousins are Biancucchi. His best friend is Scaglia. His girlfriend is Roccuzzo. The Scaglias and the Roccuzzos are cousins. Their parents manage a supermarket and share a two-story house. While Messi visited Scaglia, his future girlfriend lived on the first floor.

"Did she ever reject you?" I ask him.

The freeze-frames of Messi with a shaken expression

the instant after a mortal kick are deceitful, as are the cameras that focus on him while he moves the ball with his feet. Given the virility that soccer demands, victorious howling is necessary after a goal is scored. Leo Messi, in 2009, is the only star soccer player who is capable of touching us with his celebrations. Likewise when, at the end of a game, he puts the ball under his arm with the expression of a boy who has just won a stuffed animal at a fair. On the field, the kid loses all his inhibitions: he cries, he walks with an untucked jersey, he sticks out his tongue—he has hundreds of facial expressions. He could've given me a dirty look when I asked if his girl had ever rejected him. But Messi responds with a knowing smile. It's the gesture of someone who agrees to play.

"Ever since we met, we liked each other."

A crooked smile flashes on Messi's face.

"Then I stopped seeing my friend and her for a while. And a couple of years later, I saw her again, and, well, it started."

Suddenly, Messi turns around as if an invisible finger had just tapped his shoulder. We're ten minutes into the interview and he is already looking for the door, like the diver who counts the seconds before returning to the surface.

Others' lives seem to move slower than his.

The teacher has the same job in the same school.

The girlfriend was studying fashion design and dropped out.

The best friend plays for Greece's Panserraikos FC.

Messi grew more than fourteen inches in ten years.

Messi used to keep his ampoules filled with growth hormones in his best friend's refrigerator. He had to take them with him when he slept over.

Lucas Scaglia saw him inject himself more than once.

He had to inject himself every night.

In both legs.

One at a time.

He did it alone.

In silence.

He didn't cry.

Lucas Scaglia knew about the hypodermic needles. Yet Messi never told him he liked his cousin. Scaglia found that out over the phone, while playing in Greece, thirteen years after meeting him.

His terseness is not only reserved for the press.

"Messi only produces headlines with his feet," says Valdano.

A kind way of seeing as a virtue what the press describes as a shortcoming. Messi's silence does not come from someone absorbed in thought: it's the silence of the soccer player who makes us happy and who, happily, has nothing to add.

"So, what will you two do?" I ask Messi. "Will you get married?"

A breeze ruffles the thick summer air in Ciutat Esportiva.

"We're good as is," he responds without thinking.

And immediately follows with: "I'm not thinking of that yet. I don't feel ready at this time, and I don't want to. I think there are other things before I get married."

For the first time, Messi speaks out about the future. His words flow as if he were cautiously moving down a steep hill. It's that shy and sensible tone he uses in front of the TV cameras when he's remarking on the championship he's out to win; however, instead of goals and game strategies, he's addressing questions regarding his girlfriend and an uncertain wedding. His private life is an intriguing and well-learned story among the sports press. Yet reality suddenly interrupts his love story when a hand pops up behind his head. It's a hand with one, two, three fingers in the air. It's the club's publicity director letting me know my time is almost up. In a few minutes, Messi will once again disappear behind the walls of this big cement-and-glass incubator.

# 4

On Spanish TV, Messi's mother, Celia Cuccittini, is featured smiling in a dessert commercial that ends with Messi's childlike voice saying, "Thanks, Mom." His family and the club have created a protective bubble around him, an extension of the mother's womb where the world of rough men does not encroach upon him. Each time Messi's mother visits Barcelona, she reenacts his childhood rituals: At night, she makes him a cup of *maté* tea, she sits on his bed and caresses his hair before turning off the light. The mothers of geniuses tend to disappear off press and fan radars. To search for the woman who strokes Messi's hair is an unrewarding task. Calls always go to voice mail, which tells me her phone is off. From Barcelona, one must dial fifteen numbers to communicate with his mother in Rosario. The act of pushing each one is tedious. One night, after two months of calling her every single day, a woman finally answers the line.

Her voice sounds carefree, as if she were doing something else while answering my call.

I ask if she is Mrs. Cuccittini.

"No, I'm her daughter," she corrects me.

"I was looking for your mother."

"My mother isn't here."

"Do you have another phone number where I could reach her?"

"Yes, but I don't know it by heart."

María Sol Messi is sixteen years old and she pauses, as if waiting for me to say who's calling. She's in her house in Las Heras and explains that she's using her mother's phone because hers is broken. She doesn't appear frequently in the Messi family photos taken by the paparazzi, although sometimes she does appear in the press by accident. The day her brother was first crowned best player in the world, a television camera focused on her for a few seconds during the ceremony: She's thin and has brown hair, and her angular face gives her a slightly severe look, like her brother when he's serious. The world of soccer successes has been a part of her life since she was a little girl. When Messi traveled to Barcelona to try out for professional soccer, she was just starting elementary school.

"In the beginning, I used to watch my brother on TV and couldn't believe it," she says, out of the blue. "He is Messi, but he's still the same person. He hasn't changed."

"You watch soccer?"

"Yes, but I don't watch it with my mom. I like watching it better with my dad."

"Why?"

"No one wants to watch the games with my mom. When Leo shows up playing, she starts to scream at the TV, and she cries and gets very nervous. My father is calmer."

María Sol Messi doesn't wait for further questions to keep describing her brother.

"I'm more like Leo," she tells me. "I like staying home. With a TV and a computer, I'm happy."

"Your brother," I remind her, "told me he prefers taking a siesta."

"Yes. He gets back from practice, lies on the sofa, and stays there all afternoon. I don't know how he manages to fall asleep so easily at night. He's happy that way."

"And is his girlfriend as calm as he is?"

"No, she doesn't like to be cooped up. When Leo takes his nap, she grabs me and we go out. If you ask Leo to come out, he gets tired."

Messi's sister seems to be home alone.

His father, who also lives in Rosario, is his son's agent. Small and robust, Leo Messi will look just like him in twenty years. This year, when Barça wins the FIFA Club World Cup against Club Estudiantes de la Plata in the United Arab Emirates' capital, the audience will confuse Jorge Messi for his son during the celebration. They will lift him onto their shoulders. As a teenager, Messi's dad also played at Newell's. He had to leave the club because of military service, and later was busy with his studies and marriage. He worked in the steel industry; however, fatherhood allowed him to continue to be involved in soccer through his sons. Before Leo began to shine in Barcelona, his two older brothers played in the minor leagues.

So the business of soccer's rising star did not catch Jorge Messi off guard. But after having two soccer-playing sons, he had wished his third child would be a girl.

As a child, Lionel Messi played soccer like a marvelous flea (*pulga*)—earning him the nickname "La Pulga"—and as every marvelous flea, he did not grow. The effort to become a professional player was fueled by his desire to win, but it was also a medical necessity. When he turned eleven years old, Messi was four feet three inches tall, the height of an average nine-year-old boy. A doctor examined him, and he was diagnosed with a growth hormone deficiency—a disorder that caused a delay in his bone age. He had to receive a daily dose of somatotropin to fight it. The injectable treatment cost $1,000 a month, more than half of what his father earned back then. Soccer stopped being just a game and became a life raft that saved them from a shipwreck.

During María Sol Messi's teenage years, her brother's medicines were no longer a family issue. She now participates in her last name's fame from that invisible post that is occupied by younger siblings, those who see everything without being seen. Her brother's public life must seem like a movie, meant to be enjoyed with a big bucket of popcorn.

"One time, we were in a shopping mall, my mom, my dad, my uncle, my aunt, everyone. Leo called and said, 'I'm on my way.'"

When Messi arrived at the mall, people immediately surrounded him.

"Police had to escort him out of the building."

The way Messi unconsciously lives out his fame makes

his sister smile knowingly. Her voice is crystal clear on the other end of the line. It's not by chance that among Messi's followers, there are more kids and teenagers who play PlayStation than adults addicted to designer underwear. A year prior to this chat with his sister, in a television Q&A conducted by Argentina's former goalkeeper Sergio Goycochea, the contestant who knew the most about La Pulga's life was seventeen-year-old Soledad. María Sol Messi changes subjects as quickly as if she were flipping through channels on a Sunday afternoon.

"When he's having a bad day, it's best to not even talk to him," she tells me. "He just lies on the sofa and watches TV. He doesn't intend to be mean. He's just depressed."

La Pulga had reason to spend extra hours on his sofa: He had only scored two goals during the South Africa World Cup qualifiers, and the Argentine press kept asking where the genius was. They saw him as a foreigner with the wrong jersey. Far from his Barça routine, the Champions League's high scorer was acting like a lost and sad child. His intuition seemed to vanish; the quality that lets him do things without thinking, which, combined with his speed, makes Messi always play toward the future, one step ahead of the rest. "The quick dodge that Messi does so greatly," says writer Martín Kohan, "allows no time to think; moreover, it prevents it." Sporting the Argentine jersey, pressured by his adult obligations, Messi thought, and while he thought, he betrayed his game, where childhood irresponsibility is key. In the locker room, in that typical Argentine and Latin American culture, a leader must express leadership; you are required to be Maradona. While political leaders must gain supporters before climbing the platform, soccer leaders must win them over in the locker room before heading out to the playing field. Messi's goalless silence was starting to make some noise.

The Argentine press had never criticized him so relentlessly. They were asking him to be a strict father when he had always been a shy and mischievous son that cried from frustration. During a Champions League game, even though his team had won, Messi cried in the locker room because he hadn't been part of the starting lineup. He also burst into tears when he debuted with the Argentine team and was expelled less than a minute into the game. After winning five consecutive titles, he couldn't hold back the tears when his team was eliminated during the King's Cup. Messi lives every defeat as if it were the end of the world, with a kid's amateur spirit. However, when dealing with the frustration within his own country's team, Messi didn't cry: He stared at the ground. Instead of tears, his face was hardened.

"He wasn't well at all during that time," explains his sister. "Everyone knows it."

"And what did you do?"

"I held his hand."

Lionel Messi has the big hands of a goalkeeper.

When he was five, his maternal grandmother grabbed his hand and took him to play soccer for the very first time. Nowadays, her grandchild dedicates his goals to her by pointing to the sky. Since then, Messi does not let go of his family's hand.

"I held his hand . . . but I didn't speak to him," adds María Sol.

His brilliance pushes those around him to leave everything behind and act as his talent and fortune managers. Rodrigo Messi is the eldest of the three sons and, after his father, the second filter that must be passed in order to reach La Pulga. He landed in Europe hoping to continue his soccer career, which had began at Newell's, and now, among other things, he's responsible for making Messi's dinner. When he left the soccer fields, he studied culinary arts and is currently in charge of feeding a prodigy who wants to eat only meat on a daily basis. One afternoon, at a five-star hotel bar, Rodrigo Messi told me that his brother doesn't like fish or vegetables. That same day, he had renewed his contract with Barcelona for 10.5 million euros a year, and Rodrigo had accompanied him. He's the only family member who stayed in Barcelona to help his brother. Once in a while he gives off a nervous smile and strokes his neatly kept hair. At home, he's usually referred to by his nickname "Problemita" (little problem), and his biggest problem has nothing to do with preparing Messi's nightly dinner. It's organizing Leo Messi's security detail.

"When he leaves the house after dinner," says his brother, "I worry. He doesn't like to have bodyguards. But we place them nearby without him knowing."

"What do you think could happen to him?"

With one nervous look, Rodrigo Messi's face reveals several dangerous thoughts that he can't number at this moment.

"With fame comes envy, bad people, and we must be careful of everything," he tells me. "Soccer is another world."

Sharing a virtuoso's last name is a shadow that inspires and sterilizes you in one fell swoop. Maradona's brother was so unsuccessful in soccer that he ended up playing in Peru as if he were a circus attraction. When he played in Barcelona, Cruyff's son showed that he had only inherited his father's blue eyes. Pelé's son failed as a Santos goal-keeper and ultimately became involved in drug trafficking and money laundering. For Rodrigo Messi, the need to protect his brother in an unfamiliar and dangerous world has become his mission in life. However, at the other end of the line, María Sol prefers to talk about an unforgettable party.

"And what did he give you for your birthday?" I ask.

"All kinds of things. He was in Spain, but he called me every day," she says. "He wanted to know the color of my dress."

The soccer player who sleeps when he doesn't have a soccer ball in front of him lost sleep to celebrate his sister's fifteenth birthday. From Barcelona, he made sure that they reserved a ballroom in the best hotel in Rosario, they hired a catering service for two hundred people, and she picked out her favorite dress. He also chose the live music: cumbia and reggaeton. He gave her a gold necklace with a heart pendant and a ring.

"And did he dance?"

"Yes. And we were all surprised because he remained seated throughout my brother's wedding."

It was the first time in her life that she saw him dancing.

No one asks Messi for anything but his fantastic goals. One of his maneuvers can be a hot topic for months, and soccer lovers will one day tell their grandchildren that they saw him play. Leo Messi is unintentionally part of the special effect caused by collective happiness. Nowadays, he's his sister's hero.

"What would you like to do?" I ask María Sol.

"I'd like to go to Barcelona and study theater." Her adolescent voice sharpens with conviction. "I'd like to be like my brother one day. But as an actress."

María Sol Messi says it with the confidence of someone who feels everything is possible, challenging the precept that there's only one genius per family. She has yet to learn that behind every art hides suffering. Her brother's burden is not the boredom that lies in wait when he leaves the soccer field. With no audience or cheers, the show goes on every afternoon in Leo Messi's silent house, when he shuts his eyes and lets his head fall on a pillow.

# 5

Leo Messi prefers not to remember certain things from his childhood. Only three minutes left to the interview and he throws in the irked gesture he uses when one of his goals is disallowed: chin down, crooked mouth, and deep-set frown. It's his reaction when he notices a book poking out of my backpack. Having sacrificed his siesta is not what is bothering Messi this afternoon. Before he turned twenty-two, two biographies about him had already been published in Spain. One of them, *El niño que no podía crecer*, by Luca Caioli, celebrates La Pulga's epic journey through the larger-than-life world of soccer. Today, Messi looks at it suspiciously.

"Things that weren't supposed to be disclosed were published in that book," he warns me, as he points to the book with his chin.

Messi detests some of the episodes in his melodramatic soccer childhood. He was thirteen when he first got on a plane and flew to Europe with his father. That day, a third person was traveling with them.

"I remember it as if it were today," Fabián Soldini says over the phone.

If the trip was successful, as an agent, he would take care of the contracts. Soldini speaks of Messi with a paternal tone.

"He was so good," he insists, "that we offered to pay for fifty percent of the medicine he needed to grow."

He was a product for export and the agent envisioned his destiny in Spain.

In a home video, Lionel Messi, the boy, dribbles an orange 97 times and a tennis ball 120.

The spheres do not touch the ground.

The agent caught these magic tricks on camera.

He sent copies to his contacts in Barcelona.

"What was Messi like when he was twelve years old?"

"Very introverted," recalls Soldini. "When we took him to the doctor, he had a hard time taking his clothes off to get checked."

He also had a hard time leaving his family. During that first trip to Spain, the flight from Rosario to Buenos Aires was quite dramatic.

"He didn't stop crying," says the agent. "It seemed as if he could sense he wasn't coming back."

"He was fragile," I say. "But when he plays he seems very brave."

"Yes. He finds the challenge encouraging. He always had to play for something."

Soldini immediately responds to all the questions, as if he asked himself the same things every morning.

"Once I promised him that if he scored five goals, I'd give him a Puma tracksuit."

These were his first days in Barcelona.

La Pulga lived in a Plaza Hotel room, in the Sants neighborhood. He had left his country, where club managers refused to pay for his growth treatment. From his window he could see the Venetian Towers, the tree-lined foothills of Montjuïc, and Spain's main plaza, Plaça de Catalunya. Yet only one thought occupied his mind: He had seventeen days to showcase his abilities with the ball. In Barcelona soccer tryouts meant playing true matches. Minutes before entering the locker room, La Pulga stopped in his tracks.

"He was embarrassed to walk in there alone," says Soldini. "I had to go with him."

That afternoon Leo Messi scored four goals and had one disallowed.

The agent kept his promise and gave him his tracksuit.

Today, in Ciutat Esportiva, Messi looks suspiciously at the books that disclose that part of his life.

"So, what things should not have been published?" I ask, while skimming through the book.

"You should talk to my old man about those things," he says.

His father is startled when he realizes he has to talk shop.

"Leo never had an agent," he says over the phone. "I don't want to talk about that."

What his father does not want to discuss is a pending lawsuit. His ex-agent's company is claiming payment for the days when Soldini and his partners made sure Messi got to Barcelona. Hours invested when La Pulga's future was still uncertain. Today, Soldini's voice gets irritated when he talks about the situation.

"He doesn't even say hi to me anymore," he says of Messi. "And I had to go to a psychologist because of it. I told him: 'You didn't kill my wallet, you killed my heart.'"

Leo Messi had to adapt to the business's logic. The video where he dribbled an orange became a credit card commercial. Soldini, the producer of that childhood performance, would find this out on TV. The end of amateur innocence came with the start of his professional contract. La Pulga's first big commitment was sealed on a napkin. Barça's manager at the time, Carles Rexach, saw him play for seven minutes and, in front of a mediating agent, grabbed a restaurant's napkin and signed a commitment contract. He didn't want another club to grab Messi. Barça sealed his future on a flimsy disposable piece of paper. In less than a decade, the twentysomething went on to earn four times more than what Barack Obama declares he earns from his book sales and presiding over the most powerful country on Earth. His name is a registered trademark that functions as a family company called Leo Messi Management. The soccer prodigy has been featured in commercials for banks, soft drinks, airlines, video games, and shavers, and he's posed for campaigns in his underwear and pajamas. Pajamas he doesn't wear when taking his siestas.

Leo Messi looks over his shoulder once again but can't find the publicity director who should come and save him. His impatience is like that of an obedient student who waits for the bell to ring so he can leave. Juanjo Brau, the physical therapist who is by his side wherever in the world he may be, says that one way of understanding him is to observe the position of his head: When he lowers it, it's as if he is hanging a sign that says DO NOT DISTURB. Most star soccer players have an attitude that unites their personae on and off the field: Maradona's chest-out walk, Ronaldinho's carnival smile, Zinedine Zidane's elegant and aristocratic slowness. Away from the soccer ball, Leo Messi looks like a battery-less clone of the electrifying player we all know. A bad representation of himself. The publicity director has not come for him, and La Pulga is about to stand up; however, before doing so, he glances at his phone to confirm no one has called him.

"Do you keep your photos there?" I ask.

Messi puts on his flip-flops as if he were getting out of bed. He stretches.

"I definitely send them," he says. "But I'm not one to keep photos."

The publicity director arrives, flailing his arms like a referee who is expelling a player. It's the end. Leo Messi is no longer staring at the books in my backpack that disclose his story and that he doesn't want to read. Books, to him, are like neighbors he doesn't feel like greeting. Once, his coach Pep Guardiola gave him one. Guardiola trusted the title would be intriguing to a player who always wins. But he also hoped to send him a surprise message. It was David Trueba's latest novel: *Saber perder* (*Learning to Lose*).

"And did you read it?"

"I started to because he gave it to me," he says, referring to Guardiola. "But I don't like reading."

"Did you know it's the story of a guy who comes from Argentina and meets a girl here?"

"Yeah, I asked later and was told about it."

To know how to lose.

Lionel Messi still cries when he loses. Today, in Ciutat Esportiva, he says good-bye with a weak handshake, as relaxed and vague as he is when he doesn't have a ball at his feet. He moves and talks and goes quiet with a deceiving laziness that disappears in front of his rivals. During his golden age, Ronaldinho threw off defenders by hiding his lethal play behind a smile; Messi confuses the world with his absentminded presence. Tomorrow I will once again see him on TV, when he receives Europe's best soccer player of the year award, one of the twenty trophies he'll accept this season alone. He'll be wearing a tailor-made suit fitted just right, yet somehow still looking like it was borrowed. Afterward, he'll return to his domestic routine in slow motion—the perfect parody of the most unpredictable guy on the world's fields. However, this afternoon, Messi will drive his car, alone and uphill, to his house with a view of the Mediterranean and, as always, sink into his sofa in a hypnotic stupor.

# PART TWO

-----------------------------

## 2010

# 6

On this November 2010 morning, Lionel Messi gets out of a Porsche Cayenne and, with a slight nod, greets the commercial's producers waiting for him at Barcelona's Olympic Stadium. All the voices fade as if someone is slowly turning down the volume on the TV: Messi has to perform his ball tricks in front of the camera and he is limping. The previous day, in the Denmark cold, he had come face-to-face with Copenhagen's defenders and left with a painful expression on his face. The camera crew has come from Quebec to film player number 10 kicking the ball with fluorescent orange cleats. Messi has arrived here, at Montjuïc's side, where the view dominates part of the city, dragging his right foot. The director was hoping to capture a joyful reenactment of him scoring a goal. However, today, Messi's face is more suitable for a mattress or medicine commercial. When he walks, he stumbles and purses his lips every time he takes a step.

In a professional soccer player's life, like Messi's, doing commercials is a business commitment as, or even more, profitable than playing the game. In 2010, for the first time ever, a team of soccer players earned more than the New York Yankees, and Messi had the highest salary in the group: He earned 33 million euros, and only a third of that came from his soccer stipend. The rest was provided by commercial contracts. Soccer stars confront one another both on the field and in the fashion industry. Cristiano Ronaldo is an Armani and Nike model; Messi, Dolce & Gabbana and Adidas, the brand of shoes he is scheduled to promote with his lame foot. The Argentine is a far cry from a professional soccer player's typical proportions: His wide hips, diminutive height, long torso, and short arms require tailor-made designs. This morning, Messi arrived at Barcelona's Olympic Stadium with his brother and an image consultant who's with him whenever a camera is lying in wait. Given the contract, the commercial's producers have four hours to film him, which will result in a two-minute TV commercial. Messi's image will also be uploaded to the web by the publicists for fans to circulate. Today, as he takes off his street sneakers to put on the cleats he is supposed to promote, the reason for his limp is in plain sight. His right foot is swollen and wrapped tightly with a bandage that extends from his ankle to his instep.

The commercial's creative director is the only person who is authorized to speak to him. He's the only one on the director's team who speaks Spanish; the rest just speak English and French. But they also want to optimize the small amount of time Messi's agent has offered them in the contract. The publicity world has its own codes. Today, no one is allowed to interrupt him for autographs or chitchat. Today, no one is allowed to distract him. His right foot aches and he has to be the same hero we've seen on TV.

As a child, injuries were frequent in his life. His nickname wasn't "La Pulga" back then; it was "Enano" (midget). His shortness, combined with his speed on the field, was fatal for defenders who tried to stop him. His first injuries were always bone related. One day, before turning one, Messi followed his brothers out on the street and a bicycle ran him over. That resulted in a broken left arm. When he was twelve, a teammate pushed him during a training session and he fractured a wrist. Months after arriving at Barcelona, in April 2001, he went on the field, ready to confront CD Tortosa, and suffered his first serious injury in his career: A visiting player broke his left fibula. He spent fifteen days unable to rest his foot on the ground. He wasn't very aware of his frailty. At fifteen, in a match against RCD Espanyol, a defender broke his jaw with a header. Messi fainted. He finished that championship game wearing an orthopedic mask.

Messi's boredom when he is unable to play can easily become depression, and he isn't the only one that suffers: The sports pages turn gray and the number of heated discussions decrease at bars and offices. A soccer genius on bed rest reduces the melodrama on the field and is bad for business.

Pelé did not play in his second World Cup at age twenty-one because of extreme exhaustion that led to an inguinal sprain; Cruyff suffered a groin injury and ignored it until

the pain dropkicked him during his fifth season as starting forward for Ajax; Maradona was absent from the field
for more than one hundred days when Andoni Goikoetxea
broke his left ankle at Camp Nou; Ronaldo was injured
for three years when he broke his right knee in a Coppa
Italia final; and Zidane was a weary figure during the 2002
FIFA World Cup, played in Korea and Japan, because of
the injuries he suffered in the Spanish league. At eighteen,
Messi didn't play a Champions League final in Paris due
to a right leg injury, and he was absent from Barça's first
team for a month because of muscle tears. At the moment,
he's not a victim of his frailty, and that ensures the ongoing
soccer show business.

A soccer star always carries an obligation overload.
Unlike his teammates, Messi debuted in Barça nine days
before he underwent the required medical exam. They
needed a scorer in the little league. The managers could
wait no longer. When doctors finally examined him, apart
from the blood work and the strength and anthropomet-
ric exams, they x-rayed his wrists to measure his bone age
delay. The diagnosis held hope: With a strict diet and a
personalized exercise program, Messi could reach his max-
imum performance level without having to inject himself
with hormones. The club paid for his final growth hormone treatment. With each passing night, Messi slowly
began to wean himself off the injections.

He also stopped getting hurt. As an adult, his bone
weakness is no longer the cause of his injuries. Exhaustion
is what pushes him to the limit of what a body can endure.
After the South Africa World Cup, Lionel Messi started

an aerial marathon. He flew to Rosario (where he visited family and friends), Rio de Janeiro and Cancún (where he vacationed with his girlfriend), and Puerto Príncipe (where he was a UNICEF ambassador for earthquake victims). Then he went to Seoul, Beijing, and Tokyo to play friendly games. During his peak, Maradona played an average of forty-five games a year; in the 2010 season alone, Messi was reaching sixty matches a year. In August, as part of a tour of Asia, he had to play with Barça against a South Korean all-star team. Coach Pep Guardiola did not want him to play because he had yet to recover from last season's hits, the World Cup's wear and tear, and the lack of training during his vacation, from which he had arrived almost five pounds heavier. But the tour organizers were adamant: If Messi didn't play, Barça would earn 200,000 euros less. So Messi played. Two months later, he was called once more to play a friendly game with Argentina's national team against Japan. Fearing an injury, Guardiola refused to let him step on the field because he was still exhausted. But the business of soccer won over common sense yet again. Messi had to play. The Argentine's presence in the Tokyo and Seoul fields was worth 400,000 euros. What an administrative employee could earn in twenty years in Spain, Messi could make without even needing to score a goal or play an entire game. A match, like a commercial, is still a business commitment. To keep the industry going, they just need his image to appear in movement. And Messi didn't stop moving: In a mere ten days in August 2010, he had traveled more than twenty thousand miles—almost the equivalent of a trip around the world. "Truth is I don't know what time I live in," he said after landing in Korea. He was disoriented.

However, this morning, he's due to perform magic with a ball in spite of his painful right foot. At Barcelona's Olympic Stadium, Messi tries on different shoe sizes, and each time he puts one on, he purses his lips. Meanwhile, the routine on set moves along to the beat of a music video, as if nothing were wrong. Messi must change into the Argentine uniform an assistant has brought him. A thin blond girl hangs around at his side, dressed in a blazer and fitted black pants. She looks like a secretary, but her sole job is to put the items of clothing the soccer player tosses aside into a bag.

"These cleats are the fastest on the market," says the creative director to Messi. "Each one weighs the same as a tennis ball."

Messi listens to him in silence.

"The idea we want to portray is that since they are so light, these shoes will make you run even faster," explains the director.

Messi nods. "Where are you from?" he asks.

"Peru."

"Peru?" echoes Messi, as if recalling a landscape.

The professional world's rush skips over the protocols people use when first meeting. Television makes public figures feel so familiar that we even forget to greet them. In 2010, David Beckham's alleged lover revealed to the public that the soccer player paid 10,000 euros to meet with her. Cristiano Ronaldo made his relationship with a Russian model official before posing for an underwear

ad. Barcelona defender Gerard Piqué and singer Sha-
kira's romance was caught by the paparazzi. The cameras followed Messi and his girlfriend to the beaches of
Rio de Janeiro, where they discovered he had tattooed a
woman's face on his left shoulder blade. It was his mother's face. The second time the paparazzi reached Messi,
he was in Barcelona with his girlfriend: They caught
them leaving a Cirque du Soleil show. It was the last
time they would see him in public with her that year.
Months later, an Argentine cabaret star, who had been
with a former teammate of his from the Argentina U-20
team, published a chat where Messi asked her to pose for
the webcam. "I'm about to leave, do a little twirl." The
soccer player looked happy, as if he were about to receive
a gift. He wanted to see her full body. The scene was
recorded and uploaded on YouTube. Nowadays, anyone
who's had any contact with him may become somewhat
famous. When noticing the impact that indiscreet chat
had on the media, a reality show contestant also spoke
about an encounter she had had with Messi in a Buenos
Aires hotel room. The girl, a brunette with a stripper's
body, was moved when a TV host asked if Messi was as
good in bed as he was on the field. "Leo is a guy from
the neighborhood," she said, "and he likes girls from
the neighborhood." Given her tone of voice, it was as
if she were apologizing to Messi for the indiscretion,
for betraying his trust. Other soccer stars design their
private lives around an unattainable luxurious vibe. Yet
Messi doesn't seem to be aware of fame's dangers. At the
end of 2010, his public image as a young, disciplined, and

boring boy turned into that of an adult who sometimes acts as if no one is watching, with the naïveté of a voyeur who also forgets he's being observed.

Messi asks for a ball to play around with so he can warm up. The camera will start rolling in a few minutes, so he's invited to a trailer where there's food and a private area to rest. But he's not interested. He spends his time shooting the ball in the air, without meaning to entertain those who observe him. He dribbles the ball almost mechanically, and the ball travels from one instep to the other without touching the ground. Bobby Fischer, the first American World Chess Champion, usually carried a mini chess set in his pocket to play wherever he went. That was his way of isolating himself from the world. Instead of knights and pawns, Messi uses an Adidas soccer ball—the same one he used in the 2010 World Cup. He only stops playing to listen to his brother, who calls him from a corner. Rodrigo Messi wants to hand him his cell phone. Someone has sent a message to his Black-Berry, and for the first time this morning, a smile spreads over Messi's face.

The commercial producers have requested no one speak to him so as to not distract him. Messi's extreme concentration when he has a ball at his feet makes him seem isolated from the world. He's been a victim of his own distractions more than once: As a kid, he was late to a decisive game in Newell's minor league because he got locked in the bathroom. The second serious injury he suffered after arriving in Barcelona was his own fault: He fractured his right ankle while descending some stairs.

As with Maradona, his body only possesses athletic grace when he's in action, and thanks to TV, we can deconstruct his virtuosity in slow motion. While to other players there's nothing more motivating than posing for the cameras, the guy who leaves sports commentators speechless is happier with a text message than when starring in his own video.

# 7

Beyond the soccer bubble, the world to Messi is usually a landscape he observes from an airplane or bus window, traveling from one stadium to the next. Moreover, it's the illuminated landscape of his BlackBerry screen. The obligations required by the club take over most of his life, and chatting on the Internet is sometimes the only way he can keep in touch with friends. One morning, Ruben Bonastre, his computer science teacher, leads me to the spot where Messi took his first class to learn how to send e-mail. It's a classroom on the first floor of La Masía, the old eighteenth-century stone house, home to teenage soccer players who arrive from around the world with hopes of playing on Barça's first team. The first time Messi set foot in this house was in 2001, at thirteen years old. Bonastre was one of the first people to welcome him. He was also his academic counselor. At La Masía, teenagers attend after-school programs and learn how to compete in a team sport.

They live under a strict regimen, almost military-like, even though on the outside, the place looks like a quiet country home from another century, when Internet and cell phones didn't even exist in science fiction.

"I remember Messi rarely had his hands on the keyboard," says the computer science teacher.

"Was he lazy?"

"No. He was very absentminded and scattered," replies Bonastre. "But when I asked him to work, he tucked his hair behind his ears and acted like he was working, even though he didn't know what he was doing."

Ruben Bonastre began to work at La Masía the same year Messi came to Barcelona. He's in his thirties, with short hair set with gel and a young leader's voice. Back then, Messi's hair was long and he was just starting high school. Bonastre now understands his distraction.

"It was an intelligent attitude," says the teacher. "He knew that his main objective was to play soccer. He went to school and, although he didn't do great, he always made sure to be present. It was part of the price he had to pay."

As with almost all soccer players, the future star was never an applied student. But if he wanted to play for Barça, he had to attend all of his classes—even the boring computer science one. PowerPoint. Databases. Windows. He didn't pay attention.

Nowadays, Messi is always paying attention to his cell phone messages.

In October 2010, at his home in Barcelona, his Black-Berry rings one afternoon. It's a text message.

"You're terrible," someone says from Argentina. "I'm going to kill you."

It's Juan Sebastián Verón.

For forty days, during the South Africa World Cup, Messi roomed with Argentina's midfielder at Pretoria's high-performance sports center. They slept in parallel beds and shared the hopes of a World Cup that, in their case, ceased to exist during the quarterfinals. Verón had played in two World Cups and his tall body, wide shoulders, and bald head had become a recognizable figure in Europe while playing for Chelsea, Manchester United, and Internazionale Milano. This was Messi's first time in a World Cup starting lineup. Maradona was sure that a leader's close presence, such as Verón's, would encourage him. Given the competitive pressure, he wanted to prevent Messi from becoming that shy boy with no reflexes who had emerged during the qualifiers. Today, Verón knows how to make Messi react off the field just as he does when he's on it.

The day he welcomed me in the Club Estudiantes de La Plata dining hall in Buenos Aires, he wanted to prove it.

"Someone here is asking about you," Verón writes in a text. "Who did you send?"

Messi responds from Barcelona: "I didn't send anyone your way."

"No, dude," replies Verón. "It's a joke."

Messi is always interested in knowing who asks about his life. Verón shows me the bright BlackBerry screen: La Pulga is connected to his cell phone via chat. His image is frozen on his ex-roommate's screen. It's the typical tiny photo that web 2.0 users choose to portray themselves while chatting. In it, he looks at the camera and smiles while hugging Facha, his pet boxer. Both are on the sofa, slightly sunken on a comfortable pillow. Verón shows it to me as proof that Messi is usually connected. He likes to say all kinds of things to provoke him. However, today, amid jokes, he's also asking for Messi's permission to speak about his life.

"And does he always respond?" I ask him.

"Yes. He always needs to play and win," says Verón. "He's always looking for an incentive."

He explains it with an example.

"The other day, I sent him a text poking fun at him that said, 'You haven't written me in two weeks, what an awful friend.' And he immediately responded, 'No, sorry, I just don't want to bother you.'"

Verón opens his eyes wide.

"Bother me?" He shrugs. "He doesn't have to answer my texts."

Internet jokes can be confusing, and Messi isn't great with words.

"I know his moods, his faces, and when he's annoyed," Verón adds. "When he asks for silence, we must respect that."

"And how did you earn his trust?"

"Treating him like a brother," says Verón. And then he adds: "Or like a son."

Messi grew up surrounded by adults who were not his parents but who treated him like a son. The kid who in elementary school spoke through his six-year-old classmate now communicates with a BlackBerry, who used to take computer science classes twice a week now acts like those messenger users who are always away.

"He was here, but it was as if he weren't," recalls his computer science teacher.

Yet the Messi in the computer class was not the same Messi on a field full of soccer balls.

"The paradox is that I met with his soccer coaches and they spoke so highly of him," says Bonastre. "So you ask yourself: How is it that he enters the field with such self-confidence, yet lacks it in real life?"

In real life, after training and reluctantly attending classes, Lionel Messi spent his nights in an apartment close to Camp Nou, at the Gran Vía de Carles III. The club rents out those apartments for the families of foreign boys who come to play in the minor leagues, and Jorge Messi, his father, made sure to choose the apartment that was most convenient for his entire family. During their first fifteen days in the city, the Messi family had stayed at the NH Rallye hotel, with a privileged view of Barça's field. However, they wanted a comfortable place to settle in.

Celia Cuccittini, Messi's mother, carefully scrutinized the new apartment in silence.

"I want a house," she said, used to the quiet streets and one-story homes in Las Heras.

She didn't like living in an apartment building.

Months later, the Messi-Cuccittini family started their homeward-bound exit. The mother never managed to adapt to the new neighborhood. His second brother, Matías, was going out with a girl from Argentina and decided to go back to his country. His sister, María Sol, didn't get along with the Catalan language or with her new schoolmates. Most of them returned to Rosario. The only sibling who stayed in Barcelona was his eldest brother, Rodrigo, who opted to live with his partner in another neighborhood. Before turning into Barça's minor league scorer, Lionel Messi had been left alone with his dad in a family apartment full of empty bedrooms.

Messi told his story a decade later. "It was bad for us," he said. "There were times when my dad and I were alone and I would lock myself in my room and cry there so that he wouldn't see me." The family was unable to adapt to the city where their youngest son would become the best soccer player in the world, and while Bonastre taught him how to communicate long distance via the Internet, Messi couldn't play in any national competition because he was a foreigner. The club that he belonged to since he was a child, Newell's Old Boys, refused to grant him the international pass he needed to become a member of the Royal Spanish Football Federation. He could only play friendly games within the Catalan Football Federation B minor league.

However, FC Barcelona didn't let him go. Messi fit a sports philosophy that Barça had implemented twenty years ago in its minor leagues. The managers no longer looked for the typically tall and muscular soccer player. Technique, intelligence, and skill took precedence. When Pep Guardiola was a boy in La Masía, he almost failed to make the team because of his weak physique. His former coach, Lluís Pujol, recalls: "He had chicken legs. I didn't see anything relevant from the soccer perspective: no shots, no dodging, no arrival; not even courage or showmanship." He remembers telling Oriol Tort, who was responsible for Barça's minor leagues at the time: "I don't know what that kid has. I only see his head."

"That's exactly it," said Tort. "The kid's secret is in his head."

Investing in players with more in their head than their physical attributes caught on at FC Barcelona until it turned into the team's signature strength. When Messi arrived for Barça tryouts, he was rescued by then club sports director Carles Rexach.

"When I wanted to sign Messi," says Rexach, "some said he looked like a foosball player. I said that if foosball players were all like him, I'd want a team of foosball players."

La Pulga was part of a plan that had been conceived a long time ago.

Today, La Masía functions mostly the same as when Messi first came to town. On the cement and stone walls hang photos of old victories. The air is awash with the aromas floating in from the kitchen and the scent of the wax used on the floors and desks in the reception area. Johan Cruyff signed his first contract here, and seven of the soccer players who were part of Spain's 2010 World Cup–winning team were fed here. The rooms with bunk beds are right next to the library. Twelve students sleep there; the rest— almost fifty—live in a building next to Camp Nou. These are the same bedrooms that were home to soccer players Xavi Hernández and Andrés Iniesta, who, together with

Messi, were nominated for the 2010 Ballon d'Or. None of them is more than five feet six inches tall. Actually, when Messi first came to the club, he wasn't even five feet tall, yet everyone wanted him on their team. While playing in Cadete B, he traveled with his teammates to Switzerland, where they defeated the hosting team, FC Thayngen. During the tournament's farewell dinner, a professional soccer player went onstage to magically dribble a ball. Messi's teammates, unhappy with the show, insisted La Pulga go onstage. The wonder boy displayed an amazing amount of self-confidence with the ball that was usually invisible off the field.

"He probably didn't learn how to do logarithms," says Bonastre at La Masía. "But he did learn to get to practice on time, have coaches, and take criticism he did not like from them."

Bonastre speaks with the conviction of someone who is satisfied with his job.

"If you have self-control with a teacher, you'll have it with a coach," says the computer science teacher. "If you have self-control in class, you'll have it on the field."

Messi's discipline in the game comes from his teenage confinement. He has the cheeky skills from the Argentine field contained within the academic rigor of FC Barcelona. Born in a country made by dictators, he would have become a different type of player without the upbringing in a club based on the ball's democratization. Among forwards who defend and defenders who attack, Messi acts as a silent leader in Barça's distribution of power. However, judging from his play in an Argentina jersey, he wouldn't have won the Ballon d'Or, which crowned him as the best in the world. He wasn't able to get used to his country's team dynamic on the field. Yet it's also true that Messi's loyalty to the club that paid for his growth treatment materializes through inspired play that seems more like a show of love than an ambition to set new records.

In the South Africa World Cup, Verón had taken on the responsibility to maintain the incubator that matured Messi's genius. However, this time around, with the Argentina jersey, player number 10 was only able to shoot balls at the crossbar and goalie's hands.

"When he goes dark, he doesn't look you in the eye," explains Verón that morning in Buenos Aires. "The best thing to do when that happens is to leave him alone. Sometimes we'd get to our room and he was annoyed, and I'd let him be."

"His sister told me that when he's having a bad day, he slouches on the couch," I say. "He told me he likes to take a siesta."

"Same with me," confirms Verón. "Lots of bed time."

At thirty-five, Verón, the father of two children, likes to be in bed by eleven p.m. At the time, he was facing one of his greatest challenges: his last World Cup. Getting to bed at one a.m. was too late for him. Messi lived out his ambition with the energy of a child who's gone camping with friends. However, at home, he lies down when he has nothing better to do.

"If you let him, he'll sleep till ten or eleven in the morning. And, on top of that, he'll take a siesta." Verón says this with the smile of an uncle who enjoys his spoiled nephew's company. "The amount of time he sleeps is incredible," he insists. "I would get up, make noise, and he wouldn't even move. Nothing."

Messi used to watch the series *El cártel de los sapos*, about Colombian drug traffickers.

"He was the remote control's owner," says Verón.

While Verón acted as team captain during the games, Messi controlled the TV in their room. Javier Mascherano, one of Argentina's midfielders, was the owner of the DVDs that the rest of the players watched and shared. All of them wanted to see that series about drug trafficking.

"A lot of characters died and new ones showed up," explains Messi's former roommate. "One day Leo told me that the series was a bit dense, and he stopped watching it."

Messi was the one in charge of bringing the DVDs to their bedroom. A year before, he could have become addicted to *Lost* and *Prison Break*, but he stopped watching both before the finales.

Messi prefers to entertain himself with games where he can control the outcome.

Verón is amazed by the habits Messi maintains from his childhood. Statistics say that before a competition, a high-performance sportsperson cannot sleep more than four or five hours because of stress. When not in competition, the regular amount is nine—one more hour than people who do not practice a professional sport. According to an August 2003 FC Barcelona record, at age sixteen, Messi weighed 136.6 pounds and the night before had slept "ten hours at night and a one-hour siesta in the afternoon." Back then, each Barça minor league soccer player was required to report the number of hours slept to his coach. Messi was Barça's most skilled player and also the biggest sleepyhead in his category.

Fernando Signorini, Maradona's personal physical trainer and, during the South Africa World Cup, Argentina's physical trainer, sees in Messi an undecipherable enigma.

"The frequency of movements he has on the field is higher than Maradona," says Signorini one afternoon in Buenos Aires. "Keeping the ball so close to the foot requires an incredibly high pace. I don't know how he does it."

To Signorini, Messi is a supernatural phenomenon that came along when he thought he had seen it all.

"You see him warming up and he's as calm as a kid who's going to play on the field around the corner."

Messi isn't tense in the locker room minutes before going out on the field. He's not the only one like that; before a Wimbledon final, Swedish tennis player Björn Borg didn't even reach sixty heartbeats per minute, when the norm is more than a hundred. Signorini says Maradona showed off to distract his teammates, although Valdano recalls seeing Maradona scared, asking his mother for help before an important game: "Tota, I'm scared, help me."

"Some sportspeople are huge mood simulators," says the personal trainer. "Leo's case is different. I couldn't tell if he was worried about something. Those guys are inexplicable. They live and play their way, while the rest live and play the way others want them to."

Maradona, like Messi, was always the last one to get out of bed, as if he'd forgotten there was a game.

"Who woke Messi up in the morning?" I ask Verón.

"He'd ask the coach or me to wake him up to go to the gym. He's pretty lazy when it comes to that kind of stuff."

Being the World Cup's main figure didn't worry Messi before each game.

"Messi is the guy sitting in the corner. He doesn't do anything," explains Verón. "He doesn't put on bandages or ankle supports. He plays a World Cup quarterfinal match the same way he would play with his hometown friends."

A few days before Messi turned twenty-three, Argentina was favored for the South Africa World Cup. Although he didn't score any goals, the Barça superstar stood out on an undefeated team that kept moving forward. Two days before the match against Greece, Maradona called Messi and gave him the team captain's armband.

"I saw Leo nervous for the first time during those two days," says Verón.

The leadership responsibility did not make Messi uncomfortable. What kept him awake at night was the speech he had to give in front of his teammates.

"He spent two days wondering what to say. Leo would ask me, 'What should I say?'" recalls Verón. "And I'd answer, 'Say what you feel and it will all come naturally. But it's not easy.'"

We feel Messi is listening in on our conversation via his BlackBerry. Verón's cell phone screen lights up with an electronic dash. The dialogue with him can continue. In his chat photo, Messi smiles silently.

Maradona pressured him to speak in the locker room. It wasn't the first time he made Messi nervous. He'd had him as a guest on a TV show that Maradona hosted in Buenos Aires. He was eighteen years old and a rising star in Argentina. The show was titled *La noche del 10* (Number 10's Night). They'd constructed a small soccer field on set where Maradona, the eternal number 10, would face Messi, the future number 10. "I was in the dressing room with my dad, cousin, and uncle talking about the autographs and photos we were going to ask him for, when suddenly Diego opened the door and walked in," recalls Messi. "We were petrified. He left and we didn't ask him for anything." Five years later, amid the World Cup's competitive stress, Messi once again was petrified. During that first encounter, he'd won the mini soccer match against Maradona. Yet he still found his presence intimidating. In South Africa, the eternal number 10 wanted to motivate him by giving him the captain's armband. Before the world's eyes, the gesture seemed like a well-deserved early birthday gift. Verón, several times team captain, took it as a new responsibility: In the room they shared, he had to show the young prodigy how to act like a leader. The privilege left Messi speechless. He couldn't rally his teammates via text messages.

Three years earlier, on another TV show, Maradona declared that Messi had everything needed to be "the great Argentine player." But he also said he lacked presence.

"If he could act more like a leader," Maradona said, "I think we could go hand in hand with him to the South Africa World Cup."

"He lacks leadership?" asked the host, Marcelo Tinelli.

"Yes, presence," responded Maradona. "Because he has everything else."

Like a mirror game, Maradona hoped to see himself reflected in the image Messi projected. Messi was nineteen when he played his first World Cup, and Maradona was twenty-one when he went to the 1982 Spain World Cup. "I think that by giving Leo the captaincy, he saw himself at that same age," said Fernando Signorini. "In that match against Greece, Maradona gave the captain's armband to Maradona." In the coach's mind, Messi had never taken on the role of captain. The impact of an armband that required him to speak as a leader was bound to stress out someone who wanted to go unnoticed. In monarchist terms, successions are always troubled.

"So did Messi finally speak in the locker room?"

"He said something," recalls Verón. "But he immediately got stuck because he didn't know how to continue."

Verón chooses his words carefully. He wants to protect the team's intimacy.

"He said he was very nervous. And we entered the field."

The midfielder talks about Messi as if he were a nephew or younger brother. In the match against Greece in South Africa, the team's captaincy originally belonged to him.

"I was supposed to be the captain," says a smiling Verón. "But Maradona came to me and said, 'How about if we give it to Leo?' So I responded, 'Sure, you're the manager.' I wasn't going to go on strike because of that."

There's an emotional short-circuit when you are in the presence of an amazing act; however, sometimes it turns into pure pain. Messi came face-to-face with Verón on another field, and his friend raises his eyebrows and leans back when I remind him. It was in 2009, one night in the capital of the United Arab Emirates. The Arab public chanted Messi's name.

"Leo was annoyed that night," recalls Verón. "I know him, and I know he wasn't having a good game."

The Abu Dhabi stadium was sold out. Lionel Messi entered the field with the number 10 imprinted on the back of his fluorescent pink jersey for Barça. On the other side, Verón wore the captain's armband for Club Estudiantes de La Plata. They were playing the Club World Cup Finals; the best of the Americas was facing the best of Europe, and for Verón, who was nearing the age of a star looking to retire, it was his last chance to win the same trophy his dad accepted as a soccer player with the same club three decades ago. It was personal. Messi was after the season's sixth trophy.

"I thought, *We've got him*," says Verón enthusiastically. "I told my teammates, 'Hold on to Leo and don't let him go.' But he only needed that one second."

Messi scored the winning goal in the 2–1 victory in overtime with a shot as memorable as it was bizarre, intercepting the ball as it came plunging down toward the goal box and thrusting it into the back of the net with his chest.

There aren't many cases where players are applauded by rival fans. Maradona and Ronaldinho were given an ovation in the Santiago Bernabéu Stadium in Madrid while wearing Barça colors. Atlético de Madrid fans applauded Messi on the Vicente Calderón Stadium field, and in 2008 in Mineirão stadium in Belo Horizonte, Brazil, Messi's presence in Argentina's jersey produced a never-before-seen reaction: The Brazilian fans stood up and started chanting his name.

That hot and dry night in the Abu Dhabi desert, Messi received the tournament's best player award. Verón was the championship's second-best soccer player.

"Did Messi say anything to you after the game?"

"No, because he also knows me," says Verón. "I was frustrated and sad. He didn't even get close. And it was all for the best."

After that game in the United Arab Emirates' capital, the city of La Plata's walls were covered in graffiti insulting Messi. The guy who had hung Argentina out to dry with his scoreless performance had beaten its national team in the Club World Cup. Be it out of respect or shame, Messi didn't approach his friend to comfort him that night. He knew such a gesture could be considered provocative.

Verón sits up straight and squints his eyes, as if trying to see from afar those days he shared with Messi.

"What shames him are the stares," says Verón.

After the South Africa World Cup matches, in Pretoria's high-performance sports center where Messi and Verón were roommates, only close family members and friends could visit them: fathers, mothers, and girlfriends. They arrived in the afternoon and sometimes stayed till right before dinnertime. Messi preferred to go to his room until visiting hours were over. He wanted to avoid the crowd. When dinnertime arrived, some families always lingered in the halls that led to the dining room.

"I'd say we should go down and eat and he always wanted

to take an alternate route because he was shy," recalls Verón. "He doesn't mean harm, he's just shy."

Everyone remembers Messi as a guy who, without giving up his stardom, at times simply wants to be invisible. And sometimes he succeeds. Even with those he's shared every day of the last five years with.

In FC Barcelona's La Masía, before saying good-bye, the computer science teacher acts as a tour guide and shows me the dining hall. A woman dressed with a cap and apron is setting the tables covered with plastic tablecloths. "Today's dish is pasta alla carbonara," says Josefina Brazales. She's been serving the same balanced diet for almost twenty years, the one that Messi used to have for lunch every afternoon. Brazales is La Masía's oldest assistant. She's used to having the teenage soccer players call her Josefinita or even Mom.

"Did Messi also call you Mom?"

"No. He was very sensible and well-mannered."

In her memory, Messi is a fleeting figure.

"What I remember," she tells me, "is that he ate very slowly. He was always the last to finish and, like all of them, he didn't eat as much when we served vegetables or fish. When French fries, meat, and that sort of thing were on the menu, he sure did eat then."

Players like Messi reinforce the idea, among employees, that they are diamonds in the rough in their hands who need to be taken care of. They go above and beyond to make sure spinach or fish is not tasteless to a teenage palate. However, under Josefina Brazales's control, there are rules similar to any other school, to which Messi had to adapt. For example, it's forbidden to leave empty chairs in the dining hall, so everyone must sit as they come, in that order, and accept each day's planned menu: vegetables on Mondays, Tuesdays, Wednesdays, and Thursdays; red meat, chicken, and lamb on Fridays, Saturdays, and Sundays. Fish is served twice a week. Salad is the starter at every meal. Messi had to adjust, as all the other teenagers, to a diet where sweets were forbidden. In La Masía, they can only buy them on weekends, their only free days, during which they can spend their stipend of 50 euros a month (their sole pay from the club). The Argentine, addicted to *alfajores* (sweet dulce de leche sandwiches dipped in chocolate or powdered sugar) and *panqueques de dulce de leche* (crepes filled with dulce de leche), didn't receive that money because he lived with his father. Messi's only antidote to his homesickness consisted of every so often interrupting La Masía's balanced diet to eat croissants he received from Rosario. The rest of the time, he faithfully followed the menu taped to the kitchen's wall.

"This is like a factory," says a bald-headed man with a soccer player's name. "We make soccer players and men here."

Josefina Brazales introduces him to me while touring the kitchen. His name is Fernando Redondo. He's La Masía's cook.

"The only memory I have of Messi is that he was one of the last ones off the school bus," says the cook. "When he arrived, the dining hall was practically full."

Like someone who sees a ghost, Redondo points at a

corner table illuminated by natural light and notes that Messi used to sit there.

The table is next to an old foosball table. Josefina Brazales says the teenagers could only play after eating and on their free days. What neither she nor the cook mention is that by being the last to arrive at the dining hall, Messi could be the first to play. The strategic straggler's table where he sat to eat was number four. If there were a moral to Messi's lazy attitude off the field, it would be that sometimes the quickest way to what we really want is achieved by moving slowly.

However, the teenagers who storm in today are fast and hungry. They're coming from school on a bus that parks in front of La Masía. Redondo the cook strains the pasta and Josefina Brazales complains about the racket caused by the chairs and loud voices. Another dining hall rule is that you must behave well and no one can speak on his cell phone. If Messi were a teenager now, he would have to turn his BlackBerry off, the one he uses to communicate with the world.

"Some days, the kids get super excited and start throwing food at each other," says Brazales. "The first one I catch has to sweep the dining hall."

"Did you ever make Messi sweep?"

"Never." She smiles. "If so, I'd remember."

Then she repeats what everyone who has known him as a child says: "Messi didn't draw attention to himself."

Today, those at La Masía who wish to become stars laugh, joke around, and play like puppies. Most speak with a non-Spanish accent. Before Messi joined Barcelona's minor leagues, the number of foreign children who lived here didn't even reach 20 percent. Today, more than half of the kids Josefina Brazales cares for are immigrants. "The beginning of mankind and the future of soccer are in Africa," says Juan Villoro in his book *Dios es redondo* (God Is Round), and today, in La Masía, it seems they are living in the future. Most of the foreigners are from Cameroon. They've arrived thanks to an agreement made between the club and a soccer school founded by former Barça forward Samuel Eto'o. The assistant is touched that they call her Mom; she knows they can only communicate with their mothers through telephone or e-mail.

FC Barcelona is committed to giving minors an education and protecting them. An analysis of soccer's market figures show that around twenty thousand African soccer players have been abandoned in Europe with no legal status when the clubs that brought them from their homes ended their contracts. That is why FIFA forbids children under the age of eighteen to be transferred internationally, save for three exceptions: if the player's parents, as in Messi's case, move to the country where their child will play soccer; if the transfer takes place within the European Union or European Economic Area; or if the player's home is in a neighboring country, no more than sixty-two miles from the club that has accepted him. Today, the youngest child is an eleven-year-old from Cameroon. He's the assistant's pet. They call him "Camara," and, like other classmates (but unlike Leo Messi), he landed in Barcelona without his parents.

That said, in 2007, FC Barcelona received FIFA's Fair

Play Award. In a way, it was in recognition of an unprecedented act of philanthropy. Six months earlier, the club had signed a contract agreeing to donate 1.5 million euros a year to UNICEF during five seasons and display the organization's logo on the front of the first team's jersey.

Lionel Messi symbolizes the success of Barça's strategy to improve its club's youth team. However, most of his teammates aren't having the same luck.

"Investing in children is good business," says Bonastre. "How much will the market pay for Barça's team today?"

Bonastre knows that promoting formative soccer is a long-term investment, one that is eventually recovered. Barça inaugurated a new five-story building in 2011, in Ciutat Esportiva, to replace the old Masía, and in ten years it invested 137 million euros in the education of minors. Nowadays, if a club just wanted to buy Messi, it would have to pay 250 million euros—that equals the amount of money it would cost to produce a Hollywood movie packed with special effects. What the club cannot do, according to the teacher, is bring in a kid, not give him an education, and then tell his parents two years later that he's not good at soccer.

Messi stopped going to La Masía, as do other wonder kids, earlier than the rest. He was sixteen when he debuted on Barça's first team. Bonastre says that only 30 percent of the teenagers who come through La Masía get to work in the sports world: They become coaches, physical therapists, and aspiring managers. Two in twenty of the basic soccer players make it onto the first team, and even fewer go on to have long soccer careers. Messi, the boy remembered by the assistant as a shy teen, debuted on the first team in November 2003 at a friendly game against FC Oporto. Frank Rijkaard asked him to play, and he was the guest star in his Dragão Stadium inauguration. In the club's more than one-hundred-year history, only two players have been younger than Messi upon making their debut on the first team: Paulino Alcántara, in 1912, and Nigerian player Haruna Babangida, added to the team by manager Louis van Gaal in 1998; both were fifteen years old. After his debut, Messi decided to say good-bye to the old houseful of teens without asking permission.

"He sat at my desk and said he wanted to tell me something."

"What?" I ask Bonastre.

Bonastre doesn't remember exactly.

"I think he came so that I would ask him something. Maybe it was his way of saying thanks, no?"

In Bonastre's eyes, his most famous student's silence was a form of recognition. To Verón, on the other hand, none of Messi's texts can help delete one bad memory: having played his last World Cup with the best player in the world but without his goals. Maradona had entrusted his number 10 to the talented midfielder, but the championship resulted in a lonely Messi with bad shots.

"I don't know what he expected from me," says Verón, referring to Maradona. "Maybe some sort of support, some words of encouragement because I know Leo."

He says it with the voice of a father who has dedicated himself to educating a son, but his efforts are to no avail. It also springs from the soccer player who, close to retiring, has very little to win or lose.

On his BlackBerry's screen, Messi continues to smile curled up next to his dog on his sofa.

He has never sent his computer science teacher an e-mail or text.

Verón, from Argentina, sends him one last message.

"*Che*, you made another mistake this weekend."

Verón continues using this provocative technique, maybe to prove that his power as a leader still works. In reality, Messi hadn't made a mistake: He had scored two goals against Copenhagen. Verón just wants to get him to react.

"Yeah, I'm lucky," Messi responds, as if everything he does is mere coincidence.

Verón sends a smiley emoticon face and his phone once again goes silent. Maybe Messi is thinking of something else to add, or maybe he just decided to end the chat. It's always hard to find fun words to say good-bye, and for a guy who never knows what to say—and when he does say something, no one really remembers what it was—chat slang must be the ideal way to leave without saying good-bye.

# 8

Lionel Messi has not been a rumor factory, but anecdotes make the rounds among publicists regarding stars who have worked with him. The Argentine has the strange reputation of a celebrity who acts like just another production team employee. During the taping of a commercial for Danone vanilla pudding, player number 10 shared the starring role with David Villa, Spain and Barça's forward. They both had to shoot balls and speak in front of the cameras. Villa paid close attention to each detail explained by the director. He took two more hours than the Argentine to finish his takes. They had prepped a private room for Messi, which he refused to use, changing shirts out in the open. Throughout four hours of filming, he only asked an assistant one question:

"May I sit down?"

Today, for the Adidas TV commercial in Barcelona's Olympic Stadium, the creative director has decided to start filming a scene that involves less action; Messi is still limping. He tells him that by the end of the day, he'll rehearse takes of him with soccer balls. Messi the actor must walk to the end of the tunnel that links the locker room with the field and simulate the moment when he comes out and the audience cheers. The backlit stage looks like a time tunnel: He's wearing Argentina's white-and-sky-blue uniform, the colors he first wore at seventeen when he was unknown in his country. Today, on the concrete grandstand overhead, a group of actors and assistants is ready to represent his ecstatic fans cheering for him. Messi is a deaf man gazing toward the horizon.

"Just walk normally," says the director. "Like when you go onto the field. But lift your head," he adds.

The idea is for Messi to act focused and proud, like someone unafraid of challenging you to a fight.

"The camera will follow you from the front," explains the director. "Okay?"

Messi's lack of response causes uncertainty to whoever expects him to say more. The director doubts if the soccer player understands his instructions. Messi only wants to hear the voice that says action. His verticality on the field is a straight line that extends through the rest of his life. To score a goal or tape a commercial, he chooses the most direct path. Chatting with those who cross his path is an extra duty that overwhelms him.

Leo Messi is a flea but most definitely not a parasite. He moves a ball as if it has been sewn to his foot and forgets the rest of the world until he scores a goal. Only then does he reconcile with himself. Off the field, his shyness prevents him from sustaining a conversation. When he arrived in Barcelona, Messi took more than a year to speak with the other players in the minor league. He responded with monosyllables. He only communicated quietly with his teammates. Messi and Rafael Blázquez were inseparable. They shared Barça's Masía regimen for four years. They sat together in high school, they lunched on the same balanced diet, and they vied for the same position on the team. Messi spent his nights in the apartment where he lived with his father; Blázquez, on the other hand, slept at La Masía, where he shared a bedroom with two roommates. During the afternoons, Messi would lie down on his friend's bed to take a siesta. He didn't want to use anyone else's.

"He was embarrassed about wrinkling my roommates' sheets," explains Blázquez.

As the new guy, Messi had to pass a test on his first training day. Blázquez and three other players were asked to cover him. They had to take the ball away from the future's best player. They kicked him, but Messi didn't fall. He was a tough kid who didn't hide his modesty.

"He wouldn't finish his lunch," recalls Blázquez. "He'd ask me to wait for him because he didn't want to be left with people he didn't know."

Speedy Messi ate slowly. Like every prodigy, his upbringing involved an uneven race to tie his dazzling maturity on the field with the apparent submissiveness he shows off it. In less than five years, Messi had to prove that he could adapt to a new country, a new club, and a national team that had been the world champion twice. When he got to Spain, he not only needed to fall in step with the rigorous rules of conduct at Barcelona's La Masía. The club also required he finish his high school education. He had to score goals and pass math exams.

Sometimes Messi even forgot to take his books to class. Studying demanded more prowess than being able to dominate a ball. He went to León XIII school, where he had to learn Catalan and a teacher, Maribel Pascual, taught him French. She was his chief of studies. Messi first arrived at school with his parents and sister. At the time, Jorge Messi and Celia Cuccittini were still thinking of settling down in Barcelona. They wanted to visit the classrooms where their son would later often fall asleep and where he'd never actually get his diploma.

"They were very well-educated people," says the French teacher. "They wanted to know their son's curriculum."

Maribel Pascual has a friendly yet stern voice accentuated by the jingling of bracelets she wears on her right wrist. She's dedicated half her life to teaching in the classrooms where Messi studied for four years. For half a century, elite sportspeople have attended León XIII school, where classes must be scheduled around their practice regimens. The building has columns at the entrance and a majestic wooden staircase just inside, which give it a sacred look. Pascual's mission is to make teenagers, who think Earth is round only because of soccer, study.

"He always sat at the back," the teacher tells me, "but I made him sit at the front."

His friend Rafael Blázquez can't recall if Messi ever passed an exam. Pascual can't either. She didn't know that during elementary school, another teacher had recommended his parents take him to a psychologist. She also referred him to the school's counselor.

"When something doesn't interest you, nothing can be done," says Pascual, surrendering. "In any case, I spoke to him a lot. He has a good heart, never sarcastic and never complicated."

His elementary school teacher, Mónica Dómina, remembers him as a silent leader.

"I never saw him as a leader," says Pascual. "Messi let himself be dragged along. But if one day someone did something mischievous, he was never the instigator. He was just there."

Nowadays, Messi poses unperturbed in front of the TV cameras.

As a child, he's remembered as being invisible and moving in slow motion.

Blázquez observed him asleep on his desk from nine a.m. to eleven a.m. during class.

La Masía's cook can still see him arrive last at lunch.

The computer science teacher describes him as a sluggish kid.

The French teacher summarizes him as a boy who never did anything.

Verón remembers him not wanting to get out of bed during those focused World Cup days.

A life without a soccer ball is a tedious one for this genius player. He has a hard time moving when it comes to everyday things. A few hours before being born, the doctor told his mother they would have to speed up the birth:

Baby Messi had a slow heartbeat and it seemed his umbilical cord was tangled around him. During elementary school, because of his height, he was always the first one in line. At fifteen, Messi began to end his growth hormone treatment and the Barça coaches had a specially designed physical training program just for him. A trainer's report at the end of June 2002 reads: "He's been the player who has participated least in this job. He's been absent from twelve sessions due to problems related to his Christmas vacation and an illness. When he's been able to work, he's always been his teammates' shadow, displaying no initiative, but following form." His first public performance is a tender tribute to his slowness: In an elementary school play, the teacher decided to dress the children in costumes that reflected their personalities. Messi went onstage as a snail.

Two decades later, that kid whom everyone remembers for his slowness is now number one.

On this afternoon in Barcelona's Olympic Stadium, Messi advances along the tunnel that leads to the field with his chin up and a slight frown while a camera follows him. Colorful confetti falls like rain and slides off his blue-and-white jersey. The idea behind this take is to later reproduce it in slow motion. The director says, "Cut," and Messi once again becomes the kid who never did anything. He's silent.

"*Che*, those are cool sneakers," says his older brother, who came with him. "These are for me."

Rodrigo is the only brother who stayed behind in Barcelona to be with La Pulga during his first years in Barça. Now, he's approaching a production assistant to ask for a pair of Adidas sneakers he found in a box.

"They're samples; they aren't being made yet," responds the assistant abrasively.

The uncomfortable silence seems to grow louder.

Messi contemplates the scene without uttering a word. A knowing smile escapes him, like that of a kid who enjoys the rowdiest classmates. At a time when both talented and mediocre people are screaming for attention, Messi acts like a quiet kid who's not giving up on fun. Sometimes he even loses his sense of responsibility. The day Barça won the UEFA Champions League in 2011, the pilot who was flying the team back to Barcelona suddenly made an announcement over the loudspeaker that caught all the players' attention. During the middle of the flight, while they were all celebrating, an alarm rang in the cockpit: One of the airplane's doors was about to fly open. No one knew what had happened until a video of the party started circulating on the Internet. Among the chants and toasts with Catalan cava, you can see a hand pulling on an emergency exit handle and then a head popping up between the seats. Messi wasn't completely aware of the danger of opening that door at thirty-three thousand feet, but he wanted to see if anyone was watching him.

"We'll send you a pair to your house," says an assistant to Rodrigo Messi, regarding the sneakers he likes.

Leo Messi nods in approval. He doesn't go near the catering table they have set up for him in case he gets hungry while filming. But he is happy his brother will get the sneakers he wants.

Messi's dogged ability around the goal seems linked to his sense of loyalty. At twenty-three, he's still in touch with the adolescent friends that, according to his French teacher, were bad company back in the day. One day he called his friend Rafael Blázquez to ask where he could find a vet.

Messi tends to personally take care of the things he's interested in, and this time he couldn't solve it with a text message.

"Leo told me that his girlfriend wanted a dog," says Blázquez.

He had purchased his dog, Facha, but didn't know he was supposed to get his tail docked until someone mentioned it.

Blázquez acted like a hardworking valet so that the animal could undergo the surgery as soon as possible. Nowadays, Messi has the photo with his dog as his phone's chat image. Ten years have gone by since his friend made room for him on his bed during siesta time and stayed with him during lunch so he wouldn't have to be alone. Blázquez was expelled from La Masía for fighting with a classmate and was unable to continue his sports career. He now lives with his family on the ground floor in the Catalan neighborhood of Premià de Mar and sleeps in a room full of a mementos he's accumulated while sharing time with La Pulga: photos, jerseys, newspaper clippings, trophies. The press that covers minor league soccer said that Blázquez was La Masía's Zidane: tall, elegant, and could kick with both legs. He had a future. They said Messi was from another planet, and he quickly outdistanced his teammates. Messi stopped seeing Blázquez when they were seventeen, but he has never lost touch: He gives Blázquez his cleats and makes sure he has his latest phone number each time he changes it, and he still seeks him out for help with domestic chores, which Messi has always found difficult to handle. When Messi called to ask for Blázquez's help in finding a vet, Blázquez was recovering from an automobile accident that left him disabled. His other ex-teammates went to cheer him up at the hospital, but Messi opted to remind Blázquez that he needed his friendship. He didn't look a vet up in the Yellow Pages. Becoming a celebrity includes isolating yourself from certain domestic tasks and Messi thought his friend could help. Blázquez still feels that Leo Messi needs him.

La Pulga has been loyal to the club that gave him the chance of a lifetime and is curious about those who are loyal to him, even if it involves a stranger. Toward the end of 2010, one of his fans went to Rosario and planted himself in front of Messi's door. The guy, a twentysomething named Albin Larsson, had flown from his country, Switzerland, to meet his idol, without knowing for sure if he would answer the door. Messi greeted him and signed an autograph, and in a few hours, Albin Larsson's photo with Messi was traveling the world.

Those who know Messi are clear that reaching him is like an award granted for patience and perseverance. One night, during the South Africa World Cup, some paparazzi fashioned a pole with their tripod legs and attached a camera on one end. Like the other players on the team, Messi had rented a house in an exclusive Pretoria neighborhood. He used it to rest with his family the only day of the week he had off. His house was across the street from Maradona's and teammate Martín Palermo's. The paparazzi wanted to photograph Messi's intimate family moments on the other side of the wall. They figured they could capture a photo of Messi walking around his backyard or, at least, peeking around a door. But the invasion of privacy would only worsen things for those who waited for Messi to give them a moment of his time in person. However, one reporter's cell phone vibrated.

"Do you want to come in for five minutes and see him?" asked the text.

It was Messi's father. Marcelo Sottile, a reporter for the Argentine newspaper *Olé*, received the message.

When the journalist entered the home, Messi was next to a lit fireplace wearing Argentina's blue-and-white tracksuit. His three siblings and his girlfriend, Antonella Roccuzzo, were in the living room. Matías Messi opened the door. A soccer match was playing on a plasma TV that player number 10 did not pay heed to; he had his eyes on the cell phone between his hands.

Sottile wanted to know what everyone was asking themselves: Why was Barcelona's genius not scoring any goals with Argentina—a team that barely qualified for the South Africa World Cup?

"I wasn't myself during the qualifiers," said Messi, as if asking for forgiveness for his underachievement in the matches prior to the World Cup. "It hurt to come to my country and hear that people said I felt nothing for our jersey. Then I went to Barcelona, where I did everything fine and people loved me."

"What does being *yourself* mean to you?"

"To be loose."

The next day, the journalist published his exclusive interview and, with that, Messi managed to settle a debt. Months earlier, Sottile had been promised an interview that player number 10 canceled at the last minute. That night in South Africa, Messi was keeping his promise.

Loyalty is an act of faith that sometimes is not returned. Messi risked saying no to the Spanish team without knowing if Argentina would call him to play or not. In 2002, when Newell's Old Boys from Rosario finally granted his international pass, the following months he played in all of Barça's youth categories. He passed through the third division, then to Barça C, and, without him knowing, Argentina's talent scouts started observing him with as much interest as worry. They discovered him when Messi was sixteen and he had already received offers from Arsenal and Internazionale Milano. European clubs not only fought for his talent but also his nationality. Before he received Spanish citizenship, the country's soccer federation had already called him to train in its national minor leagues.

"When I found out that Leo could be a part of Spain's national team," said José Pekerman to me, "I became desperate."

Pekerman, former coach of Argentina's youth and adult national teams, was a soccer consultant at Madrid's CD Leganés, and he let Argentina know that Messi was about to be invited to join Spain's national team. FIFA's laws state that once a player enters the field representing one country, he cannot represent another country later on. What Pekerman didn't know was that Messi didn't want to play anywhere else but for Argentina's national team.

"Leo's family stated that their son would rather wait," explains Fernando Hierro, ex–sports director at Royal Spanish Football Federation.

Messi wanted to play for Argentina, but five months went by between Spain's offer and finally receiving a request to meet from his country's soccer federation. He was so unknown that Argentina's soccer directors weren't even sure how to spell his first and last names. The letter they sent to FC Barcelona to ask for Messi's cession refers to him as "Leonel Mecci."

The Asociación de Fútbol Argentino (Argentine Soccer Association) had had a late and improvised reaction.

"We set up a match at the last minute so that Messi could debut with the team," says Hugo Tocalli, then manager of the national youth team in Argentina. "We made it happen only for him."

A teenage Messi debuted in the sky-blue-and-white jersey on Asociación Atlética Argentinos Juniors' field on June 29, 2004; it was a friendly match against Paraguay. La Pulga played the second half and earned his place on the team: He scored a goal. Once again, he had to adapt to a new group and a new roommate. Marcelo Roffé, Argentina's youth national team's psychologist, had the responsibility of choosing Messi's roommate. He decided it should be Sergio Agüero, Maradona's future son-in-law. Roffé noticed that Messi and Agüero were living through similar situations. Everyone on the team was between eighteen and nineteen years old. They were both seventeen.

"Agüero was happy," recalls Roffé. "As if he were sent to share a bedroom with God."

"And Messi?"

"Messi made a face, as if saying, *Why don't you put me with someone who carries more weight on the team?*"

He wanted to share his room with a more experienced player.

"We told him to trust us and he understood," says the psychologist. "In the end, they were both the key to Argentina's U-20 World Cup win."

Messi roomed with Agüero until he started on the first national team. He debuted in a match against Hungary in August 2005, when Argentina was preparing for the World Cup. As he got his first touch of the soccer ball, Hungarian defender Vilmos Vanczák grabbed his jersey; Messi tried to free himself and was expelled forty-seven seconds into the game. It was an unfair expulsion and everyone saw Messi cry.

"The national team creates winners," explains Roffé. "In the youth team, one never mentions the word *champion*. We work one target at a time."

As with FC Barcelona, Argentina's youth team interprets personal success as a discipline but still aims toward the amateur ideal of just having fun while playing.

At an age when all his teammates changed habits as if changing jerseys, Messi was still stuck on his childhood behavior: humility, silence, and siestas.

La Pulga was fifteen when he received a Nike endorsement, sixteen when he debuted in a friendly match with Barcelona's first team, and seventeen when he became the youngest soccer player to score a goal in La Liga: one against Albacete Balomplié with Ronaldinho's help—his

first great partner at Barça. While his friends were gradu-
ating from high school, Maradona was inviting Messi on
his TV show.

Nowadays, among hundreds of mementos, his friend
Rafael Blázquez has a pair of F50 Adidas cleats, size 8½,
with the Argentine flag, LEO 10, and MESSI 10 embroidered on the sides. The left shoe was tailor-made to adjust
for an injury Messi suffered as a child.

It has a hole in the instep, under the smallest toe. Messi
gave these cleats to Blázquez one afternoon when he visited him while training. They hadn't seen each other in
three years.

"He was just silent," said Blázquez. "I had to pull words
out of his mouth."

That time around, Blázquez spoke more than Messi.

"He said he didn't remember our French classes."

Messi renounced everything that wasn't linked to man-
aging a soccer ball.

He repeated tenth grade in high school together with
Blázquez, but neither of them graduated.

"I suggested setting aside a special time so he could finish his studies," said Pascual. "But it was impossible: Leo
had no time left to spare."

Messi didn't talk with his French teacher again. The last
time he met up with his friend Rafael Blázquez was in 2009,
after a match between Barcelona and Real Madrid. Blázquez
waited for him in the parking lot with his girlfriend, and
Messi showed up with his. The four of them drove together
to Sants station, where his friend was going to hop on a train
that would take him to his home in Premià de Mar.

"Why don't the four of us go out one day?" suggested Blázquez.

Messi was driving. He looked at him through the rear-view mirror and smiled without uttering a word.

"This one doesn't go out," said Antonella Roccuzzo. "The only thing he does is sleep."

Blázquez remembers Messi being as silent as he is generous.

"He always went to school with a Sprite in hand and coins in his pocket to invite me out."

He loved sodas. His gum had to be mint flavored.

"Leo always smelled good," says Blázquez. "Like fresh air. Like a boy who's always clean."

Nowadays, Messi looks tired. In Barcelona's Olympic Stadium, on this 2010 afternoon, he must simulate the focus he has before a game. That's the theme of the next shoe commercial scene. Messi is sitting on a wooden bench facing the lights focused on him. The taping, this time around, is in the locker room, so he doesn't have to use his sore right foot.

"What do you do in the locker room before going out on the field?" asks the director.

Messi is quick to respond. "I chew gum."

The director was hoping to create the supposedly solemn mood that should be present in a locker room before a game. Now he seems to prefer to give him instructions.

"How about you just put on a serious face and look ahead."

On the monitor, there's a close-up of Messi surrounded by semidarkness. In the camera's eye, with a sudden spot-

light on his sparse beard, he looks like a gladiator prep-
ping to enter an arena. The publicist envisioned him as a
hero facing the world. In the locker room's loneliness, his
image could also be that of a kid who slowly outdistanced
his friends until he was left to face his audience's demands
alone.

# 9

Messi is embarrassed when his family and friends comment on his rebroadcasted games on TV. That's why he prefers not to watch. He tends to act as if he were dodging his own image: He wears discreet brand-name sportswear, and although he changes hairstyles two or three times a season, his bangs immediately look the same as when he was seven years old. No matter what he does, he always goes back to being that unkempt kid who didn't tuck in his shirts. It's the image of one who prefers to forget mirrors. But one night, he was unable to avoid meeting a guy who introduced himself as his official double. It was after a game; when he entered Camp Nou's VIP room, filled with actors, politicians, and reporters who had come there to meet the players, he bumped into a human caricature of himself. Miguel Martínez, a Catalan twentysomething whose job is to refill cigarette machines at bars, has played Messi's double in soft drink, cell phone, and airline ads, as well as a Chinese search engine commercial. He told Messi he was his body double and wanted to say hi.

"I wanted to tell him about how people react when they see me," says the double to me one morning at his house. "The things they say to me on the street."

The double has a larger, aquiline nose and he's two inches taller than Messi, but he has the same relaxed walk and kicks the ball with his left foot. When Messi saw him, recalls the double, he was surprised and uncomfortable.

"He wasn't effusive. That made me take a step back."

In 2010, Lionel Messi was a cloning candidate. When he was crowned the best player in the world, he turned into the perfect spokesperson to push any product, and his image was endlessly reproduced on TV and the Internet. In one of these commercials, which his double keeps on his cell phone, there's a scene that features Messi with drenched hair, heading a ball violently. The drops of water jump against the backlight in slow motion. The fake Messi presses *pause* in the middle of that move and claims that's him. There are takes that require the precision only Messi can deliver, but the superstar wasn't going to risk his health filming a night scene with soaking wet hair. That's when his double steps in, earning up to 12,000 euros per job.

Sometimes Messi appears in the least expected way. One morning a crowd saw him come down in a helicopter and land at Hackney Marshes, the meadows west of the London. A few boys playing soccer nearby ran toward their idol as soon as they saw him. Messi kicked the ball around with them briefly, then hopped into a car heading toward Hanbury Market, better known among Londoners as Spitafields Market, a wide commercial area with designer clothes, organic produce, and cool Indian restaurants. The whole trip was part of a publicity stunt. Messi was presenting new shoes, and the ad campaign was titled *Catch Him if You Can.* The goal was for fans to arrive on time so that Messi himself could give them each a pair of shoes. However, the person who didn't make it on time was Messi. At Trafalgar Gardens in Tower Hamlets, some fans insisted on waiting for him. Traffic issues delayed his arrival. Messi was tired, and when he finally arrived, he didn't approach them. His supporters were only able to catch a glimpse of him through the car windows. His double wasn't with him that day to take over.

A soccer player's useful life span lasts around twenty years, and the hope of having Messi for twice that long doesn't only belong to the fans and publicists. The soccer industry, like the fashion business, looks for replicas. Anxious to see kids from the Argentine fields, Catalan soccer experts with the green thumbs to grow talent do not wait for a new prodigy to show up through middlemen or his parents. If Argentina produced world soccer stars such as Alfredo Di Stéfano, Maradona, and Messi, logic indicates that the next genius in line could originate from the same place.

FC Barcelona crossed the Atlantic in search of the future's soccer player.

"Messi's status boosted this project," explained Jorge Raffo, a former player for the Boca Juniors who's on a mission to find the new Messi.

He's the director at FC Barcelona Juniors Luján—

Barça's La Masía branch in Buenos Aires. This center offers training and housing for soccer players under sixteen years old. It's located in Boca Juniors' old headquarters, La Candela, on the southwestern tip of the city, in San Justo. Raffo's greatest challenge is to reproduce the FC Barcelona model in a landscape of low houses, thin dogs, truck fumes, vehicle repair shops, and deep potholes on dirt roads. Barcelona is a distant skyline. The trainer has a Barça badge sewn onto his T-shirt.

When Messi left for Barça, Argentina was on the verge of collapsing into its longest financial crisis in recent history: The equal exchange rate disappeared, the government restricted the withdrawal of private money from banks, and the country had five presidents in one month. One of the consequences was the suspension of some national services. For example, welfare and national health insurances that covered somatotropin in the past—the synthetic growth hormone Messi needed to grow—stopped covering that medicine. His father had to find help in soccer clubs to continue his son's treatment—Newell's Old Boys only collaborated for two months, River Plate denied its support; now Barça is the club that Messi states he will never leave.

Raffo has spent five years searching for another diamond in the rough in a country where soccer is still an escape from poverty.

The day I was heading to Buenos Aires' La Masía, newspaper headlines announced that meat and gas prices were due to rise more than 10 percent. The truckers' union had organized a demonstration that stopped traffic and ended with a police officer killing one protester. Soccer helps you forget everything for at least ninety minutes, and Buenos Aires' La Masía is an artificial island smack in the middle of the storm. The training center is housed behind a steel gate that opens up and reveals a picture-perfect postcard featuring an English-style cottage surrounded by fields of freshly cut green grass, locker rooms staffed with kinesiologists, and a restaurant with a special nutrition-based menu. In another building, the teenagers have their bedrooms with private TVs, and each day they follow a routine that replicates what Messi's was like in Barcelona during the early years.

"Messi was uprooted and had to suffer those consequences," says Raffo while showing me the place. "We want to prevent other kids from having to live through the same pain."

The trainer believes the teenagers must first go through an adaptation process before leaving for Spain; that's why life at Argentina's La Masía simulates Barça's routines. The aspiring Messis wake up at six a.m., go to school, have lunch at La Masía, and, in the afternoon, form pentagons on the field. They kick the ball forward and look for the surefire pass, following Messi's footsteps. Then they attend tutoring sessions. Every September 11, they celebrate the Diada Nacional de Catalunya, and they sing "Els Segadors," the Catalan anthem. Adapting to the Catalan model more than nine thousand miles away is not only for sports training. Today, the director of Buenos Aires' La Masía has two hundred teens under his care. They hail from poor neighborhoods in twenty Argentine provinces. Most have never seen the big city before.

The youngest player is nine years old. Around 40 live at La Masía and another 150 come and go from their homes. They all understand that being a disciplined soccer player is not enough; they must also learn how to negotiate their future.

"We are mercilessly battling agents," assures Raffo. "We believe a kid does not need one until he's no longer a minor."

Their current agent is FC Barcelona itself. These teenagers are under the same financial agreement as those in Barcelona's La Masía: They sign a contract backed by their parents. Raffo summed it up as follows: Barça owns federative rights as well as financial ones, and keeps 50 percent if a player is sold to another club. In exchange, they offer the kids an education, housing, and the possibility of being part of the best team in the world.

To the children at the Argentine La Masía, Messi is a role model they watch on TV. There's a photo of him taped at the end of a staircase that leads to their bedrooms. The image shows a group of them posing with the star. Ever year, FC Barcelona chooses ten players from this Buenos Aires branch to travel to Camp Nou and practice on its training fields. The kids weren't able to meet or take pictures with their idol on this trip. However, as a consolation, they were photographed with a cardboard Messi at the entrance of the stadium's souvenir shop. (Messi's double is often used by tourists to trick their friends into thinking they actually met him.) The adolescent soccer players, however, don't joke around. None of them mentions, unless someone asks, that the Messi in the photo is not real.

Of almost five years of work at Buenos Aires' La Masía, only one player was invited to transfer to Barcelona: Maximiliano Rolón, the closest they've come to Messi's brilliance. He's fifteen years old and also a Rosario native. He doesn't have a double, but he does have a twin brother who attended La Masía. The less fortunate twin didn't make it to Spain and was sold to the Argentine club Vélez Sarsfield. The players Barça rejects are transferred to local teams. Maximiliano Rolón had to part ways with his twin brother to overcome the hardest test that these adolescents must face if they want to take the leap into European soccer: bidding their family farewell.

"The boy is alone," recalls Raffo.

Messi was accompanied by his father, who stayed with him in Barcelona. Maximiliano Rolón landed in a limbo similar to millions of immigrants: Any Argentine with a visa may stay in Spain for three months, and Barça's La Masía takes advantage of this legal time frame to try the possible new Messi on the field. There are minors who attend other club tryouts with no guarantees. According to UEFA, five thousand foreign minors have ended up wandering the streets of Italy after arriving in hopes of starting a career in soccer, and each year around a thousand talents originally from Brazil and Argentina lose contact with their parents after traveling to Europe with the promise of a contract. According to immigration records, Rolón is a tourist who entered the country as if he were visiting an uncle. However, the reality is that he has crossed the ocean to face the strict father represented by FC Barcelona.

The price to reproduce Messi's story is always high.

Barça spends 1 million euros a year searching for his clone in Argentina, and the results of five years of hard work have been lackluster. The club's president visited Argentina's La Masía halfway through 2011 and anticipated he would have to close down the branch. Soccer is a business, and when the managers initiated this project in Argentina, they never imagined the cost-benefit relationship would be so uneven. La Masía in Buenos Aires would have to shut down due to lack of funding. Maximiliano Rolón was not only the first but also the last player to leave Argentina's field and make it to Barcelona. Nowadays, he is still playing for the club. His talented teammates back home will keep playing for the Argentine clubs that bought them. Others will be stuck in the process Raffo called "adaptation time." Each of them knows he will not be like his idol, even though he had the opportunity of a lifetime at his fingertips.

One person whose career timing was on point was Messi's double. The morning he welcomes me to his home, he introduces me to a girl with dyed platinum-blond hair. He says he met her thanks to being Messi's double. What does it feel like to be Messi's girlfriend without really being Messi's girlfriend? In his bedroom, he keeps all the FC Barcelona jerseys he's used since the beginning of his career in Spain. A duvet embroidered with Barça's insignia covers his bed, and he tells me he can reproduce every one of Messi's facial expressions.

"I don't cut my hair because Messi's hair grows incredibly fast."

He doesn't change his look until he's hired to shoot

a commercial. Sometimes, groups of tourists pay him to act as Camp Nou's tour guide. When asked for an autograph, Miguel Martínez uses Messi's distinct signature: the stretched out *M* that covers the rest of the last name's letters. However, underneath it, where the star usually writes "Leo," the double writes his first name.

"I let older people know I am not Messi," he tells me in a scrupulous voice. "But I can't tell kids the truth. I don't want to disappoint them."

Messi doesn't like to see his own image on TV, while his double enjoys posing for the cameras. The producers immediately thought of him for one of their most important 2010 commercials, featuring the fluorescent orange cleats that were filmed in Barcelona's Olympic Stadium. The double had to run with a ball at his feet while the camera recorded him from the waist down. He's acted as a leg double in some takes. However, there are last-minute changes to the plans.

"Messi doesn't want Miguel Martínez to be his double," says the director.

Just like Messi, his double is also a small-town boy; resembling the best player in the world changed his life. TV shows began phoning him to talk about soccer and he'd go. Nowadays, he gives any journalist who approaches him an interview. His Facebook profile reached the five-thousand-friend limit a while ago, and he frequently gains access to and receives free drinks at the city's happening nightclubs. He spent his last birthday raffling off Messi's shirts in exchange for drinks at nightclubs Messi never attends.

"His double became very popular," explains the commercial's director. "Messi didn't like that."

He was out of the recording.

They had to find another leg double.

No soccer player expects his double to do more than a basic approximation of his own gestures. Zidane's double is an Argentine who moves with his same grace. Maradona's double has raised his arms at public events pretending to be the legend himself. Beckham's Spanish double has the same tattoos and is younger and more muscular than the original. To someone like Messi, who avoids watching his own image on-screen, he might find it amusing to see his caricature in fun house mirrors. Like in Disney World, where it doesn't matter if you take a photo of yourself hugging a stranger disguised as Mickey Mouse, soccer fans don't care about taking a photo with a Messi who's not the real thing. They know they'll probably never get to meet him in person and they want to be as close as possible to the star. It's what happens at a wax museum with a movie legend. Admirers demand their idols have an unflappable image where they can deposit their hopes and faith. Messi doesn't want to disappoint his followers, even though he's a myth in the making. The twenty-three-year-old, whom the fashion and soccer industries hope to clone, still tries to change his childlike hairstyle, which refuses to disappear.

# 10

Lionel Messi gets annoyed when he's treated like a kid. In a few minutes, he must act in the most important take for the shoe commercial, and his face shows a skeptical and heated expression, as if they'd just called out a foul he didn't commit: He raises his eyebrows and chin and *tsks* with his mouth. He arrived on set limping, but the pain in his right foot isn't what's overwhelming Messi this afternoon: It's the director's words. They are in Barcelona's Olympic Stadium surrounded by the film crew. Messi looks put out.

"I asked him to aim at the camera and kick."

Messi must take a more than sixty-five-foot kick. Professional soccer fields aren't like the ones we see on TV; they look huge in real life, and it seems impossible to control the ball's direction within those dimensions. The kick is not simple; Messi's foot hurts and the director is only interested in getting the star to perform well for the take.

The camera is set in one of the goal's right angles, between the crossbar and the post.

"I asked him if he was capable of making the shot," explains the director.

What annoyed Messi was that question.

Feeling that someone doubts his skills makes him uncomfortable.

It's not the first time something like this happened.

Messi joined the world of camera flashes when he was seventeen. His father explained that it was time to transform his image into a commercial product and he took him to a restaurant close to Camp Nou, where they met with an agent.

"He was just a child," says Rodolfo Schinocca to me in a Buenos Aires bar. "I remember he ordered a hamburger."

At that time, Messi had already debuted on FC Barcelona's first team and was a substitute for Argentina's national youth team. Schinocca was an accountant and former player for Boca Juniors who agreed to invest time and money to help publicize Messi. The agent had played defense in the mid-eighties, and from those days, he still has a bowlegged walk and a short, sturdy body. He was only able to play seven matches with Boca before he was forced to retire due to an injury, but he continued in the soccer world as an agent. La Pulga was his first client.

"Believe in our son," he recalls Messi's father telling him. "He will be a great player."

"Was it hard to sell his image?"

"The business needed to be overhauled," said Schinocca. "At the time, the image of a successful soccer player was David Beckham."

Messi was a teenager with acne, and his agent could've tried to change his look; instead, he highlighted his adolescent features. His first clients were McDonald's, Lay's, PepsiCo, and the Argentine electrical appliance store Garbarino, where anyone could purchase the video games Messi was so addicted to. Although he was unknown in Argentina, his agent decided to feature his first commercials in his home country rather than Spain. That's how La Pulga became known as the kid from Rosario who was finding success in a foreign club.

"He was very humble," recalls Schinocca. "He always said to me, 'The only thing I want is to have a house in Barcelona and another one in Rosario.'"

Shy Messi had to act in front of a camera. His first TV commercial was for a soft drink. It was filmed on a set in Munro, Buenos Aires. Schinocca was with him. They were taping on a field with an uneven lawn and, to break the ice, the producer challenged him.

"I bet you aren't able to juggle the ball so that it bounces off the crossbar instead of making it into the goal."

He had to do this three times, in exactly the same way.

"So did he do it?"

"Yes," says Schinocca. "But before doing it, he asked, 'What are we betting on?'"

Messi had faith in himself. He wanted to bet on something.

At the time, he still lived alone with his dad in the apartment provided by the Barcelona club. His mother and siblings drove a Fiat Duna around Rosario, and they all flew economy class with layovers in Rio de Janeiro, London, and Rome. It took them more than thirty hours to get to Barcelona from Buenos Aires. It was the cheapest solution for a large family. Entering the advertising world would mean flying first class. On that afternoon when he faced the cameras for the first time, Messi accepted the producer's challenge: He bet twenty cases of soda.

He only had three chances to make it.

"The first time," said Schinocca, "he missed."

The ball bounced twice off the crossbar and Messi lost control.

The second chance came around, and he bounced it fourteen times.

On the third try, he bounced it twenty times.

After winning twenty cases of soda, Messi had to star in his first scene. He had to receive a ball that came at him from the air, jump, and execute a scissors kick. The ball had to hit a red dot that the director had painted in the middle of a piece of glass. The idea was for the glass to break as evidence of the impact's strength.

At the Buenos Aires bar, Schinnoca remembers that moment.

"On the first try, the ball veered off path. 'It's gonna be a long day,' said an assistant on the sidelines."

That comment offended Messi.

With the next kick, he shattered that piece of glass.

The director said that was enough.

Messi asked that they set up another piece of glass.

He broke it again.

"It's an insult to defy him with a ball."

Schinocca recalls the incident with raised eyebrows.

On this afternoon, six years later, at Barcelona's Olympic Stadium, Messi once again gets ready to shoot a ball at a camera on the field.

Suddenly, one can hear glass and metal shattering.

Messi has blown away the camera in one fell swoop.

The director now has to film another take and adds: "Now please aim at the camera without hitting it."

Messi laughs softly. He doesn't like people confusing the brilliant soccer player with the shy guy who seems fragile off the field. The producers weren't sure if he'd be able to bear the pain in his right foot through the end of filming and figured if they explained each scene in detail, they could avoid doing too many takes, and he wouldn't have to force himself too much.

Messi repeats the kick with laser precision and the scene is finished in less than half an hour.

He's wearing Argentina's jersey. The objective was to capture a new version of the goal he scored in a 2010 friendly against Spain's national team in Buenos Aires' El Monumental. That afternoon, Messi appeared to the left of Spain's goal and delicately raised the ball over the goalie. It was a subtle shot. Argentina won 4–1, and the commercial's production team filmed the whole game. They were going to use those images in the shoe campaign. However, Messi's original, subtle goal simply didn't do it for the director. He wanted a stronger and less delicate shot. That's why he decided to turn real soccer into a movie.

"Could you play around with the actual shoes?" asks the director.

He must display his prowess with the shoes. The idea is for the orange shoe to jump from one instep to the next and then shoot right toward the camera, slightly grazing the lens. That clip would then be uploaded to the Internet so that users can send it to each other, hopefully going viral.

The only condition is that he must film the scene in socks.

"Do you think you can do it?" asks the director.

Messi raises the shoe with the tip of his foot, but when the plastic sole hits his right instep, he grimaces.

"Want to try it again?"

"I don't know," he mumbles. "Let them decide."

Messi points to his brother and image consultant, who up until now were just mere spectators.

The director just keeps mentioning that the main characters in this story are the shoes.

Messi has to be an acrobat with his throbbing foot.

The story on TV does not reflect reality. "The greatest passion of our time is not soccer, but televised soccer," says Juan José Sebreli, an Argentinean historian and philosopher. A game is always a story told by the cameraman working for the mass of TV viewers. The South Africa World Cup final, for instance, was seen live in Johannesburg's stadium by close to one hundred thousand people, while almost 1 billion viewers watched it on TV, where the main character is always the player who has the ball. In televised soccer there are no time-outs. Most of Messi's admirers only know him from watching him on TV.

This afternoon, the commercial's director not only wants to construct an audiovisual story of the genius we are used to seeing in action, but he wants to turn him into a superhero.

"If his foot hurts," says Rodrigo Messi, "he's not doing it."

The older brother demands Leo be allowed to do the same dribbling tricks with another object. The shoe is too hard.

Someone appears from behind the white lights with a tennis ball.

Messi makes the small ball jump around without hitting the floor for more than twenty seconds and he kicks it toward the camera.

A few weeks later, this scene will make its way around the Internet. But instead of a tennis ball, Messi is playing with a fluorescent orange shoe. The video producers replaced the tennis ball using digital technology, and Messi looks like a circus juggler.

However, the real Messi is a sweaty laborer who earns his keep by scoring goals. He changes shirts in front of the whole production team. The same blond girl remains by his side, putting away the clothes he's worn in a bag with the speed of a ball girl. The girl does nothing else.

"It's happened to us before," explains the creative director. "If someone else takes it, we run the risk of it showing up on eBay."

Fetishism toward Messi is the most intimate act of admiration on behalf of his fans, and even though he's no longer an innocent and amateur icon, his followers continue to see him with childlike cheer. It's the morbidness in adults that causes them not to recognize that they enjoy watching Disney cartoons, that they prefer a fantasy-filled soccer game versus the manly sport involving strong legs and long kicks. Among the more than two thousand objects linked to Messi that are auctioned off on the Internet, photos of him posing with Mickey Mouse are still up for grabs. He donated the white cleats he used during the 2010 season to a Catalan toy museum.

Early talent tends to be profitable, and La Pulga began to generate seven-figure numbers at an age when he didn't even have a driver's license. In 2005, he signed a contract with FC Barcelona, an unprecedented move for a kid his age. He was set to earn as much as what Carlos Puyol, expert Barça and Spain defender, earns today; or the same as then Atlético de Madrid forward Sergio Agüero: 5 million euros a year. Messi's soccer talent was immediately associated with the value of his image, and a year after that contract with Barça, two sports brands contested his sponsorship in a lawsuit that ended in court. Messi received a counteroffer to the 100,000-euro preliminary agreement he had signed with Nike; Adidas was willing to offer fifteen times more. Hence, Messi opened up a teenage market that was previously nonexistent within the professional soccer industry. It was the first time the two sports brands competed with each other for a soccer player, and the highest bidder won.

"Did Messi change when he started to earn money?" I ask his agent.

"He never changes," assures Schinocca. "When he had enough to buy a Ferrari, he bought a gray Mini Cooper."

He then clarifies: "Yeah, he obviously did things kids his age would do. He'd tell me he wanted to go out with a girlfriend after the game and asked me where to take her."

"Was he popular with the girls?"

"Being introverted lets him get closer to women," says Schinocca. "Leo conveys trust."

Schinocca smiles, as if remembering a joke. The mischievousness in shy people, like Leo Messi, is hard to explain without being indiscreet.

In 2005, La Pulga traveled to Pereira, Colombia, with his agent to play on Argentina's youth national team in the South American Youth Championship. His mother and father also accompanied him. Messi was a sub and roomed with Sergio Agüero. Schinocca mentions that at the end of a press conference with the players, one TV reporter said she wanted to meet Messi and gave Schinocca her phone number.

"The next day, I took the girl's number to practice," continues Schinocca, "and he said he had already been with her."

The agent chuckles knowingly.

Messi went unnoticed when he didn't have a ball at his feet. But there was more to him than his shyness.

"One day he escaped from the house," says Schinocca, "and his mother called me."

He was going out with a girl from Buenos Aires who was a film major and TV producer. At the time, he needed to focus on practicing with the national team. He was preparing to travel to the 2006 Germany World Cup and wanted to be with his girlfriend before leaving.

It was his first time with Argentina's national team, and his parents wanted to keep him safe at his Rosario home. But Messi dropped off the family radar.

"His mother called me angry," says Schinocca. "She said it was my fault that Leo had taken off because I had lent him my car."

Messi had taken refuge in the InterContinental Hotel in Buenos Aires. Schinocca went to pick him up and take him to Ezeiza's sports center, where his national team-mates were training.

That was the last time Schinocca and Messi spoke face-to-face.

Earlier, Messi found Schinocca packing his suitcase. His agent told him he wouldn't allow his mother to blame him.

Messi said to pay her no mind.

In less than two years, the agent had sold Messi's image to promote soft drinks, potato chips, gas, fast-food restaurants, desserts, and electronic appliance brands, and he had negotiated his first contract with Barça. Schinocca was able to garner success as an agent that he was unable to achieve on the field as a soccer player. But the business relationship ended six months after the Adidas contract was signed—the sports brand that now had Messi starring in their soccer cleats commercial.

"We had a meeting in Buenos Aires," says Messi's father, referring to Schinocca, "and I told him that it was the end of the road for us."

When Messi turned his last name into a commercial brand, Schinocca was an inexperienced agent full of ambition. Messi's parents were new to all the business dealings. They signed a contract for commercial rights adding Messi's mother as director, and they created a company under the agent's name. The agreement began to unravel when one afternoon Schinocca sent one of his employees to Messi's house; he had some papers his parents had to sign. That day, Jorge Messi was in Barcelona and his wife, Celia Cuccittini, signed a company amendment written in English, where Schinocca awarded most of the player's shares to himself. With this move, Messi's father would be a smaller shareholder in his son's representation. He felt swindled and he refused to comply with the agreement. The agent sued him.

"If you ask me if I thought Leo would earn tens of millions, I'd say no," says Schinocca. "Definitely a million."

La Pulga just wanted to own a house in Rosario and another one in Barcelona. Nowadays, his parents and the agent have a pending trial and a countersuit for fraud that amounts to more than 8 million euros.

Schinocca lowers his voice.

"I know I won't generate another player like Messi," he says. "If I even think about that, I'd have to jump off a balcony."

During the last year, apart from being a commercial image, Leo Messi began to turn into an exemplary benefactor: He agreed to be one of UNICEF's goodwill ambassadors and, together with his father, created a foundation that sponsors a soccer school in Rosario, supports welfare projects for minors, and inaugurated a hospital specializing in the treatment of Chagas' disease. From time to time, in Africa and the Americas, soccer saves talented children from misery, and they become millionaires and turn charity work into a feature of their career. Samuel Eto'o, former Barça forward, also founded soccer schools in Cameroon. The Argentine player Carlos Tévez has donated heavily to Fuerte Apache, the shantytown in Buenos Aires where he grew up. Both of them preserve the hardened and defying spirit of someone who has suffered in order to make it. Leo Messi, however, always appears with a halo of goodness.

Now, Messi must speak when a camera goes on. In the Olympic Stadium, the filming of the shoe commercial is close to ending. Messi takes the Argentina uniform off and puts on a blue tracksuit over his jersey. They are going to tell him what to say.

"Please," says an assistant, "just look into the camera and ask: 'What would you have been if you hadn't been a soccer player?'"

The director explains that the question is directed to David Beckham. The English soccer player is also in the commercial. The idea is for the main characters to have a conversation.

Messi remains silent.

"We already have Beckham's answer recorded," explains the director. "We just need your question."

"But I don't care what Beckham would've liked to be."

Messi's silence doesn't mean everything's the same to him.

Guardiola understood this in 2009. The team was ready to practice one morning in Barcelona's Ciutat Esportiva, and Messi hadn't shown. They thought he was sick. They later learned the truth: Two days earlier, Guardiola had not played him in a game against Sevilla and Messi was offended. The coach wanted to save him for a more important match in the Champions League. What Guardiola didn't realize was that the Argentine player doesn't accept not playing ball. Messi rejects being a supporting actor on the field. He never plays a character that is not himself. If he doesn't agree with the script, he responds with a tense silence. Guardiola never kept him from playing again, and he fired the forwards who were challenging Messi's position: Zlatan Ibrahimović and Eto'o. Messi was the Champions League striker for three seasons. His goals are also a way of expressing his silent opinion.

Fast-forward back to 2010. Messi refuses to speak to Beckham on a TV screen.

"It's only part of the commercial," insists the director.

The image consultant asks him to wrap it up.

During the following months, Leo Messi will appear on the Internet dominating an orange shoe with his feet. No one notices the bandage underneath his sock. For now, he moves listlessly toward Barcelona's Olympic Stadium exit, where his Porsche Cayenne awaits him. He has the same expression he had when he arrived at the set with his aching foot, the face of a star who greets everyone with his head down. But now he walks loosely toward the light that invades the stadium and lets everyone see he is no longer limping. The director smiles suspiciously. It's the knowing smile of someone who feels he was played and believes that today the best player in the world made up a sprained foot.

# PART THREE

--------------------------

## 2011

## II

During the afternoon of January 10, 2011, Lionel Messi appears in Zurich's Park Hyatt hotel lobby believing he is bound to lose that night. The city's Kongresshaus is the place where the Ballon d'Or will be awarded to the best player in the world, and he thinks the prize will go to one of his Barça teammates who won the World Cup the previous year. Switzerland is one of the least soccer-inclined countries in the world and also the place where, once a year, the prize for the world's best player is awarded. Messi has arrived with his mother, uncles and aunts, a cousin, and his sister. He had been celebrating Christmas and New Year's with them in Argentina. Today he's wearing a Dolce & Gabbana tuxedo with a four-button vest, a satin lapel, and a pleated bow tie around his neck. Messi walks across the high-ceilinged, wood-paneled room, stops in front of a table with drinks and traditional Alpine sausages, tries a sip of champagne, and then sits on an ivory-colored sofa. From one minute to the next, amid more than fifty people from Barça, he remains seated as if he were alone. It's the fourth time he has traveled to Zurich as a Ballon d'Or nominee. He was last season's winner and triumphing again would mean joining a list whose sole entry is Johan Cruyff, the only player to receive the award even though he lost that year's World Cup. However, in his progression of successes, Messi hasn't wanted to repeat his wardrobe.

"Leo," intrudes a man with an Argentine accent, "why are you wearing a bow tie?"

A black limo waits for him outside the hotel.

The Ballon d'Or's red carpet has served as an elegant way to retire early. Ronaldinho had been crowned the best in the world in 2005, and when the smiling ambition that drove him to his highest point disappeared, his fall from greatness began at Barça. Before the appearance of Wayne Rooney, English soccer's last great hope had been Michael Owen, who in 2001 was also regarded as the best, but after the party, he disappeared from the headlines, as well as the clutches of would-be gold diggers. The Brazilian, Ronaldo, who at twenty-one was the youngest player to receive this award, eventually turned his brilliant trajectory into more injuries than goals, although he still managed to receive a second Ballon d'Or. The pressure behind early recognition can also kill ambition, produce broken ligaments, and turn winners into fleeting stars. "It's my first death," said Ronaldo in 2011 when he retired from the fields. Soccer is an epic drama that today, in Zurich, the Argentine contemplates as if he were watching a bad movie.

Messi remains seated in the lobby, watching other

Barça players talk in front of the TV cameras and glance sideways to diplomatically avoid fans. Never before in its one-hundred-year-plus history has FC Barcelona received so many awards as it has during the last few seasons when Messi has been a starting player and Guardiola the coach. Seven of the players on Spain's national team, which would be named best team, were also part of his club, and even Guardiola traveled to the event as a best coach nominee. The Ballon d'Or verdict, a ruling that involves more than 450 experts—all the national team coaches and captains and more than ninety journalists from around the world—is an honorable piece of news, in spite of the distance created by the formality of the event. This afternoon, Messi seems immune to the solemnity, playing hide-and-seek with his fans, who have fooled hotel security, among men in suits, women who have a hard time walking in heels, and some children who give the gala an intimate, wedding-like feel or that of a first communion. His two teammates, also in the running for the Ballon d'Or, accompany him in silence: Andrés Iniesta, whose parents came by train because they're afraid to fly, and Barça's second captain, Xavi Hernández, who approaches the ivory-colored sofa when he realizes the Argentine is still sitting there, alone with his BlackBerry. Playing soccer is a way to continue living your childhood. Today, Messi has found a way to go back in time without a ball by childishly using the phone as his shield against the fans in the hotel.

One November afternoon last year, Leo Messi sent several text messages to a friend via his BlackBerry.

"We should organize a New Year's Eve party," he said in the first text from Barcelona.

The message went to Juan Cruz Leguizamón, a former teammate from Newell's minor league. They met when they were six years old and to this day are still friends. La Pulga was the scorer and Leguizamón was the goalie. He welcomed me to his home one day in Rosario and instantly connected with Messi through BlackBerry chat. He wanted me to read their conversation.

"When I get there, I'll call you," continued Messi, "and we can organize the whole thing."

The messages arrive on his BlackBerry like a harp's melody.

Juan Cruz Leguizamón is the same age as Messi, but he looks older. He's used to screaming out orders below the crossbar and that goes well with his hoarse blues singer voice, although it is contrasted by his dreadlocks. Sports chroniclers call him "Rastafari" Leguizamón.

"Coming here grounds him," he tells me, referring to Messi. "He sees people, he takes his mind off things. It's good for him to know we'll all be together again."

Each time he goes back to Argentina, Messi has dinner with his friends, a group that he's known since elementary school. One of them is his best friend, Lucas Scaglia, number 5 on Newell's team. Juan Cruz Leguizamón was in charge of stopping the balls that Scaglia missed. Both of them live in the same neighborhood and organize the ritual that usually goes like this: buy meat, charcoal, and wine and drive to Roldán, a neighboring town where Scaglia's parents have a house with a barbecue and a soccer field. Leguizamón tells me about this while Messi follows our conversation from his cell phone.

After losing the 2010 World Cup, Messi told the press he wanted to go home. In truth, he was only going to be in Argentina for a week. The plan was to travel to Rio de Janeiro with his girlfriend. Before leaving Rosario, he organized a barbecue with his childhood teammates.

"Leo is the shy friend, but he's always available. If you ask him to go to such and such place, he'll come. And if you let him, he'll always pay."

All Messi can think about that afternoon is inviting his friends to a great big New Year's Eve party.

"When you get here we'll have the party," confirms Leguizamón through another text. "An all-inclusive barbecue."

"Yes," responds Messi. "With hookers too."

The message is frozen in the middle of his friend's screen. Messi's chat photo no longer features him smiling next to his dog. He's now posing next to his eldest nephew, his brother Matías's son.

Leguizamón responds quickly, but Messi is faster.

"First we have to barbecue and then we'll deal with the hookers," he jokes from Barcelona. "Worst-case scenario, we throw them in the river to shut them up, ha ha ha."

The friends laugh in unison. Private chats between friends should never be published.

"He's coming for a week and wants to do everything he doesn't do in a year," he says.

Spain doesn't air out the intimacies of Barça's wonder boy. But in Argentina, the paparazzi chase after him when he's in Buenos Aires. Sometimes they wait for him at a building in the Puerto Madero neighborhood where Messi has an apartment on the thirty-fourth floor. Other times, they stalk him at entrances to hotels he usually visits. They want to snap photos of him with women.

One of them was a TV model who once danced at a strip joint for Bill Clinton. She went to the InterContinental Hotel and was with Messi. She would later say she left the room quickly because the soccer player refused to pay her. She tried to charge him $2,000. Gabriela Vitale, Juan Sebastián Verón's ex-girlfriend, had introduced them, as she works in public relations, often with TV women who are looking for fame and for famous soccer players who have fantasies about these cabaret stars. Vitale introduced the model to Messi, assuming they would come to an agreement.

"Leo is a great friend," Vitale says to me over the phone. "Each time he swings by Argentina he asks me to introduce him to the girls on TV."

Messi had met her at a dinner in Buenos Aires. Vitale was already someone in the entertainment world and had appeared on TV many times, showing off her curvaceous figure with silicone breast implants and speaking in a girl-ish voice. But she became most famous when the police confiscated her cell phone in mid-2011. They were investigating her links to drug trafficking, and among the text messages that implicated her in a drug-trafficking case were texts from Lionel Messi. He said he got excited just thinking of her.

"He's very young," says Vitale during our conversation. "Any guy that age wants to meet famous women."

Messi returned to Buenos Aires in July 2011 to play the Copa América. Before training with his team, he called his friend. His relationship with his girlfriend had ended.

"He was hurting from the breakup," says Vitale, "and with that impasse, he made the most of it and went out. He's a bit more awake. He's into having fun."

Messi has left the image of Barça's pampered field boy behind. He's starting to look more like the partying soccer player stereotype, except he doesn't drink alcohol. "The young Amadeus," says the writer Martín Caparrós, "is many steps closer to becoming Argentine, and now he could really threaten Maradona in his own territory." It wasn't the first time the two were compared. In 2007, Messi scored two goals identical to ones made by Maradona, and the world thought he was his reincarnation, although the older number 10 scored both against the English team at the 1986 Mexico World Cup, while Messi did so against Getafe CF and RCD Espanyol in the Copa América. Setting the goals aside, Leo Messi's public image is closer to Maradona's this year, a lighter version strengthened by the desire of an Argentina that longs for the myth.

"He prefers to be seen as dumb rather than horny," says Vitale. "One can never see his desperate face. He's like a fifteen-year-old kid. Mischievous yet embarrassed."

In his country, Messi searches and does not find his past; it's a comfortable, anonymous intimacy. To some, he's still a guy with an average aim on the national team who's shown he has renounced his origins. Coming to Rosario is the equivalent of experiencing the place where he prepares his future. He still owns his childhood home in Las Heras, and during the past few years, he's bought a children's soccer school, a bar across from the grove that borders the Paraná River, some apartments in the highest building downtown, and a cottage with a pool in the town of Arroyo Seco, a peaceful area only forty minutes from the city. On the land where the Argentine flag was first raised, across from one of the ten most important harbors in the country, and close to Che Guevara's birthplace, lie the offices of the Fundación Leo Messi and the family company, Leo Messi Management, set on the eleventh floor of a building with a mirrored façade. His father manages his son's fortune there.

"One photo, Messi, just one photo," pleads a blond man at the Hyatt.

Sitting on the sofa in Zurich, Messi knows he can't hide from his fans behind his cell phone any longer. Two blonds sit in the center, extending their arms over the Argentine's shoulders as well as his teammate Xavi Hernández's, and they all wait for the muffled digital click. Before saying good-bye, the tallest blond does something else: He puts his hand on his neck and winks at Messi. It's the second comment regarding the idol's bow tie. Not many feel the need to say something about a tie; however, a bow tie tends to have a fun factor when worn by a gifted soccer player who's twenty-three instead of an exceptional orchestra director. His early consecration is represented by the bow around his neck that highlights his present success and seems to announce his future triumphs.

"We weren't used to losing," said Leguizamón that afternoon when he welcomed me into his home in Rosario. "When we lost one game, we all cried."

Messi's first team, known as the "87 Machine" because of the year the players were born, rarely won with less than five goals. They traveled all over Argentina and were crowned champions at an international tournament in Peru. Messi still holds the record of having scored more than one hundred goals in thirty games every year. La Pulga was the children's club's engine, steamrolling in a city where soccer passion is only comparable to the visceral rivalry between Boca and River. The Rosario fans intimidate with a fierceness that goes beyond their names: The Newell's Old Boys followers go by the name of Los Leprosos (the Lepers) and Rosario Central fans are known as Los Canallas (the Riffraff). The mutual hate that unites them also makes them indifferent to other national league teams. Messi moved to Barcelona when he was the leader in Newell's minor leagues. To those who met him, he never stopped being a Newell player.

The training fields where Lionel Messi was formed are called Islas Malvinas (Falkland Islands) and have such sparse grass that only the most dedicated goalies will dive on it. Juan Cruz Leguizamón is still the winningest goalkeeper in the history of Newell's minor leagues. Sometimes the hardest conditions make those who survive them preserve an essence that causes them to be better and more resilient. La Pulga comes from one of the most competitive fields in Argentina: six- to twelve-year-old children are divided into six categories, and every weekend around three hundred child soccer players compete to become professionals. That same club also gave birth to world soccer stars that any Newell's fan could list by memory:

Gabriel Batistuta, Roberto Sensini, Abel Balbo, Marcelo Bielsa, and, of course, Valdano. To reach Barcelona, Messi survived incredible childhood competition on a dirt field.

"The problem we have here," says Ernesto Vecchio, "is that we get very thin kids because of malnourishment."

Vecchio coached and trained Messi before he moved to Spain. He still occupies the same position in Newell's today and, with almost thirty years of experience, he's the oldest coach in the club's minor league. He has a thick mustache stained with nicotine and owns a car repair shop, which has always been his main income. He works at the club three times a week and just this year began to earn a salary. Before then, he did it for free.

"Leo was small, but he wasn't malnourished," explains Vecchio. "He didn't get tired, he steadied his legs and took the hits."

Vecchio clenches his weather-beaten fists as if he were dealing with boxers rather than soccer players. Messi was the fighter with ID number 99231 and played in three categories simultaneously. During weekends, he'd finish one match and a few hours later start another one.

"His father always stood behind the goal," recalls Vecchio. "He never got together with the other parents."

At an age when children mimic what they see at home, La Pulga was an obedient forward.

"Messi had a good family environment," he adds. "But usually one of his teammates' fathers brought him to the games. His dad never could."

His father worked as full-time supervisor at Argentina's most important steel mill. His mother, Celia Cuccittini, had quit her job at a magnetic coil factory to take care of the children. María Sol, the youngest in the family, was still a little girl who required all of her attention.

Vecchio's best years in the minor leagues were when he had La Pulga on his teams.

"Messi was everything on the team," says the coach.

Today, Juan Cruz Leguizamón is Central Córdoba's goalie, a Rosario team playing in the Primera C league, the fourth division in the Argentine soccer league system, and Messi is still the VIP passport that makes his old teammates privileged guys. Player number 10 preserves his relationships with his childhood friends, and once in a while, he makes sure to reconnect with group outings, although now that they're men, the trips are more adult. During the past holiday season, he invited all of them to Madame, a Rosario nightclub that claims to be the largest one in South America. In front of the VIP room where they were stationed, a line formed of people who wanted to greet the idol. Each time Messi went to the bathroom, he had to do it with a group of bodyguards. Navigating the crowd alone was nearly impossible. Leguizamón observed the spectacle as a supporting actor with a movie star.

"And to think we had almost forgotten about Leo," says the fourth division goalie.

When Messi moved to Barcelona, he didn't send any news from Europe. He didn't have an e-mail account yet. His friend remembers he remained silent for three years and his old teammates thought he wouldn't come back. However, his self-imposed solitude was necessary for a player facing a trying situation. Messi was adapting to FC

Barcelona's strict rules. To his childhood friends, his image remained that of the kid they used to call Enano, who had to inject himself with growth hormones every night. Juan Cruz Leguizamón purses his lips each time he remembers that image.

"If you looked at his legs, you could see they were covered in needle pricks, but we didn't have a clear idea of what it was," he says. "We were young, and you aren't as aware at that age. We just wanted to play."

When Messi came back from Barcelona, he was also only interested in playing. In his three-year absence, he had become a soccer player sponsored by Nike, who was about to be called to join Argentina's national team and who had already received offers from prestigious European clubs. Messi was aware of what he was worth and he was beginning to make a name for himself in his country. He had waited to sign his first contract as a professional soccer player before reuniting with his friends. Barça accepted him and hence, before his friends' eyes, he was still the small leader who didn't like to lose. They saw him on TV as he raised a World Cup trophy for Argentina's U-20 national team and watched as he received his gold medal in the Beijing Olympics. When the national team played in Rosario, Messi got all of them tickets. He wanted them to see him playing live in the starting lineup. That winter night in 2009, Argentina's national team faced Brazil in the South Africa World Cup qualifiers. Maradona was the head coach. The match took place in the Gigante de Arroyito Stadium to a sold-out crowd. During the second half, Verón passed the ball to Messi. They were losing

2–1, and he had the chance to tie this classic game. Messi looked for space; two Brazilians were covering him and they slipped the ball out of his control. That was the last he would see of the ball. There was a long shot and within seconds Brazil scored 3–1. Messi was crestfallen. He didn't know that apart from his friends, his childhood coach had also come out to see him play. Ernesto Vecchio was there, but he wasn't able to get a ticket, so he went to the stadium's entrance at the end of the game. He hadn't seen his most memorable student in ten years.

"I waited for him until I saw him leave on a bus," says his former coach. "He was sitting down, in another world, staring straight ahead."

Messi hadn't played like the kid Vecchio had trained. He didn't want to return and be defeated in his country, yet that night Brazil won in his own hometown.

"I flailed my arms hoping he'd notice," says the coach.

"Did Messi see you?"

"Yes." He smiles under his nicotine-stained mustache. "He blew kisses my way."

He didn't see him again. Messi, a player who doesn't like to lose, returned to the club that couldn't afford to pay for his growth hormone treatment and lost. He donated 22,000 euros to help equip Newell's facilities, which still flood when it rains. It was a form of gratitude; a way of sharing his fortune with his childhood friends.

When Messi invited Juan Cruz Leguizamón to a New Year's Eve party and joked around with him through BlackBerry chat, his friend received and responded to his messages as if he were involved in some sort of mischief.

It seems like his life accelerates when he's with Messi and quiets down when he leaves. In his living room, he only has one photo of both of them posing together and smiling. Among the mementos the goalie treasures, the most valuable one is not a jersey or a pair of his cleats. It's not even an unforgettable goal. When a guy makes his fans see his brilliance as a routine, his absence becomes as memorable as his biggest plays. The game Juan Cruz Leguizamón remembers the most is one where Messi hardly played.

His team was losing by two goals.

He was the goalie.

"Leo arrived at halftime," he says.

They were playing a championship final and the winning prize was bicycles. Messi had been mistakenly locked in his bathroom and came running to the game his teammates were losing. He had broken a window to get out.

That afternoon, the team won by three Messi goals.

Each of his teammates went home with a bicycle.

Juan Cruz Leguizamón is wide-eyed as he remembers this event and suddenly jolts his head up, alert. It's another message from Messi.

"Leo is asking me your name," he says, and shows me his BlackBerry screen.

After finalizing the New Year's Eve party details, Messi wants to know who is asking about his life. He doesn't seem to mind organizing a party in front of a stranger. His friend doesn't care either. The goalie quickly types my name then tells me he has to go: His mother tells him lunch is ready. As if he were still the kid who played with Messi to win a bike, the goalie gets up and goes to the dining table as if he is about to receive a great award. After the South Africa World Cup in 2010, journalists asked themselves how a professional like Messi could still cry when he lost. "Messi is still playing for the bike," suggests Mexican writer Juan Villoro.

The bicycle is still spinning to this day. It has high mudguards that make it look like an all-terrain motorcycle. On this afternoon, in Zurich's Park Hyatt hotel lobby, Messi must get into a limousine that will drive him to the Kongresshaus to hear who's crowned the best. No one else is asking for his photo, but it still seems he'd like to be invisible, if that is at all possible while wearing a tuxedo and being Messi. His black suit's bow tie and his humble demeanor remind some of a waiter.

"Mr. Leo," says one man, raising his voice. "Please get me a Coca-Cola."

Gerard Piqué, Barça's defender, makes sure to use a millionaire's snobby tone. Their teammates David Villa and Carles Puyol laugh. Messi imitates a server's posture, smiling and lowering his head. It's hard for him to find a comeback with public jokes. He doesn't seem to be aware of what he represents, or maybe he just feels insecure today. In the soccer world there's an unspoken rule in Europe that is respected every four years: The Ballon d'Or winner, with the exception of Cruyff, must have also won the World Cup that year. Proof of this are the cases of Bobby Charlton in 1966, Paolo Rossi in 1982, Lothar Matthäus in 1990, Zidane in 1998, Ronaldo in 2002, and Fabio Cannavaro in 2006. Messi had received his first trophy when he was five years old, and this afternoon in Zurich, he acts almost like a guest to his team's stars. Ceremonies tend to feel endless to him and a far reach from the past's security, where matches were won only to have fun. Messi has worn a bow tie even though he thinks he will lose.

# 12

Lionel Messi never leaves Rosario without stopping at the house where he lived till he was thirteen years old, which today is mostly uninhabited. Sometimes he leaves as soon as his neighbors find out he's visiting. The rest of his days are spent at his cottage about eighteen miles from downtown Rosario. The woman at the kiosk across the street from his house says that there are weeks when none of the Messi family comes by, so she recommends I look for his grandparents. Las Heras is a working-class neighborhood in southern Rosario and no one drives by here unless they live in the area or they are Messi admirers who are in town and think they may find him by buzzing the intercom. A sign taped to the mailbox warns that the bell doesn't work. This isn't the only house belonging to the Messi family. The second one belongs to his paternal grandparents, Eusebio Messi Baro and Rosa María Pérez Mateu. They've lived here since they were young and nowadays work at a bakery. Apart from their clients, the grandparents do not welcome many guests. The rest of the Messi clan also doesn't visit much.

Biographers obsessed with understanding genius's DNA are usually drawn to grandparents, but no one else remembers a famous soccer player's grandparents. The streets where the stars grew up take precedence in these cases. Villa Fiorito became famous because of Maradona. No one knew about Três Corações until Pelé arrived on the scene. In soccer's biology, the neighborhood's influence is genetic manipulation. Johan Cruyff lived five blocks away from the De Meer Stadium, home of AFC Ajax, the club where his father provided fruits and vegetables and where he debuted in the first division. Las Heras, Messi's neighborhood, is made up of only a dozen square blocks next to what used to be military barracks. It's one of those neighborhoods where coins are important and houses are only one story high. The house where Messi grew up is the tallest one in Las Heras; it has a second story with a balcony, an air conditioner, and four closed windows facing tree-lined streets where the neighbors greet one another by name. La Pulga's parents and grandparents were Las Heras neighbors before getting married. The wives of his older brothers also lived in the same neighborhood. His maternal grandfather, Antonio Cuccittini, is a widower and still lives in Las Heras. The only grandmother Lionel Messi mentions in public is his mom's mother, Celia Olivera de Cuccittini. She took him to his first soccer match and passed away when he was ten. Now player number 10 pays tribute to his deceased grandmother by looking up at the sky when he celebrates his goals.

The grandchild, like most, isn't close to all his family members. Eusebio Messi Baro's house is two blocks away from his, but his paternal grandfather looks like a relative removed from the world of success associated with his name. The house has a metal door and, next to it, an open window. Eusebio Messi Baro improvised his business: What used to be his bedroom is now a bread and pasta shop. The metal eyeglasses that mark his nose reveal a fragile man, although he will soon turn eighty-five and has a body that resembles a gnarled tree. He has huge hands like his grandson; however, unlike him, he offers a handshake as firm as pliers. Eusebio Messi Baro keeps his accounts in order with a pen that he carries in the pocket of his shirt, which is worn out at the collar and cuffs. He lives there with his wife, and his house connects to his daughter's patio—Gladis Messi, a woman with dyed blond hair, Messi's least-seen aunt.

"I haven't seen him in over a year," she tells me as she opens her door.

There's resignation in her remark, as if Messi's absences are normal. Absence is familiar territory between grandparents and grandchildren. On the wall hangs a newspaper's front page with a photo of the grandson raising the U-20 World Cup trophy, which he won with Argentina. Next to it, there's a Virgin Mary postcard. The rest of the living room is inhabited by a table covered by a plastic tablecloth with a pepper, garlic, and onion pattern, as well as a yellow canary in a white cage, a TV, four chairs, a narrow staircase that leads to the floor above, and a bed with a headboard and stirrup similar to those used in hospitals. The wall paint is cracked and the lighting has been reduced to one yellow bulb. It doesn't look like the home of grandparents who gave birth to Lionel Messi's father and agent.

The grandmother, wearing a purple rosary around her neck, watches us from the edge of the bed. A Sunday afternoon comedy is playing on the TV. Laughter can be heard in the background.

"It was a year and a half ago," recalls the grandfather. "Leo was about to get in a car in front of his house."

The soccer player had traveled to Rosario on vacation, and when he stepped out, a group of fans huddled around him. He had to escape into that car. That was the last time his grandfather saw him.

It's true, grandparents usually complain that their grandchildren don't visit. Messi's grandfather says that he wasn't able to come say hello because he couldn't get through the crowd of people.

"I don't even think he was able to see me," he says.

Messi began to distance himself from his childhood streets, but he didn't neglect his old house: He built a second floor and a garage and restored its façade. His paternal grandfather had set the foundations before he was even born. Eusebio Messi Baro grew up in the countryside, in a nearby town, and then migrated to the city of Rosario. He worked in construction and transportation and bought the land where he himself built his home as well as the soccer player and his siblings' home. Messi's grandmother cleaned houses. The bakery is a business she started some time after he was born.

The grandparents say that their grandson spent most of his time on the Las Heras streets. La Pulga and his siblings, apart from playing on the streets, trained at a local club called Grandoli, where Messi stepped on a legitimate soccer field for the very first time. His grandfather sometimes picked him up in the same truck he used for work. He drove him to his practices. Messi's dad started driving him when he joined Newell's.

The grandfather smiles and talks with his hands.

His wife, on the other hand, is serious.

"But during the time Lionel's injections were happening, they were destitute," says the woman from the bed.

Her voice is loud but confusing, as if she were chewing her own words.

Rosa Pérez Mateu recalls when her grandson had to inject himself with growth hormones and the treatment cost more than half his father's pay.

"Well, he had to support four children," says the woman as she clutches a handkerchief near her mouth.

Sometimes grandparents say things that disclose too much information or embarrass their children and grandchildren. A few months after my visit to Las Heras, Antonio Cuccittini, Messi's maternal grandfather, was the one who exposed his grandson. "Leo doesn't have a girlfriend now. He had one but they got into a fight," he said on the radio. "And he's better off now; he's too young." Cuccittini was referring to Antonella Roccuzzo without realizing that his grandson never speaks about his private life in public.

Grandparents keep memories we forget. This afternoon, in Las Heras, Messi's paternal grandmother remembers him as a child who would stop by the bakery to ask her for a few coins.

The grandmother raises her voice, revealing a mouth missing teeth.

"I helped them with bread and milk. And now look how they repay me."

During the last few years, Rosa Pérez Mateu has broken her arm, elbow, and hip. She can no longer climb the stairs to her bedroom, so she had to have a bed placed in the dining room. She had surgery on her legs, and her teeth have become weak. She says that the pensioners' public health insurance doesn't function properly.

"But now my son is going to start paying our property tax," interrupts the grandfather. "That's a huge help."

The grandmother glances to one side.

The neighborhood where Messi was raised acts like a big family. There are only a few last names in Las Heras: Arellano, Jiménez, Vallejos, Quiroga, Barrera, Cuccittini, Messi. The woman who works at the kiosk across the street from Messi's house has Calcaño de Quiroga as a last name. She is a widow with one daughter. Neighbors stopped buying at other kiosks to help with her income. Once, a neighbor's mother breastfed Leo Messi.

"We used to say we were cousins," says Cintia Arellano from her porch.

Lionel Messi was born a month and a half after her, and only a wall divides their backyards. A while after giving birth, Celia Cuccittini realized she didn't have enough milk to breastfeed her son. Cintia Arellano's mother fed her neighbor's son when she needed to. Since then, she recalls, both families say they are "belly" or "milk" friends. At elementary school, Messi always sat with his neighbor; she was the girl who acted as his interpreter and helped him communicate with his teacher when he was too shy to speak.

Cintia Arellano grew up in a neighborhood cabdrivers avoid, where walking alone at night is not recommended. Similar to almost all of their neighbors, the entrance to the Arellano family's home is separated from the sidewalk by a floor-to-ceiling gate. Las Heras is no longer the peaceful place Messi left behind when he moved.

"I always picked him up to go to school and asked him if he liked any girl," says Arellano. "But he never fessed up."

"His teacher," I remind her, "told me that you spoke for him in class."

"It's that he was so shy and small . . ." She smiles. "I always raised my hand for him."

Messi abandoned his studies to dedicate himself to soccer; Arellano is majoring in psychology and is a special-needs teacher for children. She has brown hair and speaks in the unhurried tone of people who know how to listen.

"I felt I had to protect him," says Arellano. "Those types of kids always caught my attention."

She was the second person in the neighborhood who recommended I visit his grandparents.

"Where do you think he gets that absentminded and calm nature?" I ask about their grandson.

Eusebio bends his rigid body and sits next to his wife, on the edge of the bed.

"I think it's from his dad," he says, slightly doubtful. "He's very serene when speaking."

The grandmother, however, quickly responds.

"His wife is more nervous," she says of Celia Cuccittini. "She's the one who has the control."

The feud between mothers- and daughters-in-law is a family folklore staple. The classic phrase "Behind every great man is a great woman," applied as a compliment toward women, contains, ironically, the essence of this fight. Alexandre Dumas, Sr., wrote in one of his novels of a police captain who barks out the same order every time he receives a complaint: "Look for the woman." Instinctively, he believes she will get him closer to the truth. La Pulga has a portrait of his mother tattooed on his back. Behind Messi's father, a woman can also be found, but it's not his mother.

The grandfather stares at the ground.

She takes advantage of the silence. "So, what's Barcelona like?" asks the woman.

Eusebio Messi Baro's grandparents were Italian. Rosa Pérez Mateu's parents were Catalan farmers. The grandmother complains about not visiting the land where her parents were born and where her grandson reaps the rewards of success.

Lionel Messi's life shares some episodes with the lives of great Argentine myths: a humble origin and an illness, abandoning home at a young age. It's the story of Evita, El Che, Carlos Gardel, and Maradona. "Most universal Argentines," warns writer Martín Caparrós, "had to stop being Argentine to become Argentine." Messi first garnered recognition outside of his country, and now he's welcomed home as if he were a messiah. His neighborhood has no monuments or signs with his name. The only visible altar is dedicated to a secular and miracle-working saint. Here, neighbors pay tribute to Antonio Mamerto Gil Núñez, the Gauchito Gil (the Foolish Little Gaucho), a livestock driver who was sentenced to death for deserting the Autonomist Party, the Liberal Party's opponent in the nineteenth century. His cement statue, featuring him in wide pants and a gaucho hat, is located at the corner of Messi's house. Beneath a mulberry tree, neighbors care for him and hope their prayers will be answered. Before having his throat slit, Gauchito Gil asked his executioner to pray in his name to save the life of his own son, who was sick. After killing him, the executioner kept his promise and prayed in the name of Gil and his sick son was cured. Since then, believers worship that miraculous paternal gesture.

The last time neighbors waited for Messi was in front of his house. He had won the U-20 World Cup. The neighborhood was welcoming home the future Maradona. He just needed to grow.

His friend Cintia Arellano was in charge of collecting donations to buy paint, paintbrushes, and fabric. "We waited for him till five in the morning," she explains. "When he arrived, Leo was trembling with excitement."

Player number 10's personal life is an enigma. She discreetly leans forward when speaking of a secret. Messi not revealing what girl he liked at school wasn't the only thing he kept from her. She found out he injected himself with hormones when they were about to embark on an end-of-year school field trip to Villa Carlos Paz, a city in the Córdoba Province on a lake and surrounded by mountains. They were going to spend a week together. Cintia Arellano's mother was accompanying them. The woman received a special request before leaving: Cuccittini, her neighbor, asked if she could take Messi's hormones and make sure he injected himself every night. That was how Arellano discovered he suffered from a growth hormone deficiency.

Visiting Las Heras is like stepping into the past.

His family paid for a telephone line three months ago.

There's still no sign of it, and they have no Internet access either.

The company that provides this service takes a while to get to this neighborhood.

Cintia Arellano doesn't exchange e-mails or text messages with Messi. Las Heras remains an analog world with grandparents who will never leave. La Pulga was eleven years old when he first left the neighborhood without his parents. He did so to visit his maternal grandmother's grave—the one he dedicates his goals to. It was a spring Saturday. Messi wasn't alone. A neighbor was with him.

"Leo insisted he wanted to go to the cemetery," Diego Vallejos tells me.

Messi didn't offer any other explanation. That morning, they hopped on a long-distance bus and paid close attention so as to not miss their stop.

Diego Vallejos has always lived on Messi's street. They went to school together, and that trip was his first time leaving the neighborhood as well. Today, he works at a tire factory and wants to put together a rock band. He has dark skin and long hair. He plays a blue guitar stamped with a photo of Messi wearing Argentina's jersey. Messi's grandmother was buried in Villa Gobernador Gálvez, a town thirty minutes south of Rosario populated by shacks, uncovered waste pipes, and stray dogs wandering the dirt roads.

"I told him we should go back," says Vallejos, "but he wanted to keep going."

Two eleven-year-old kids looking for a cemetery: Messi had assured him he knew the route, but halfway there, they got lost. Up until then, their most daring plans had included venturing over to a street vendor alone and buying hamburgers, and exploring the mysteries of a building under construction. Before visiting his grandmother's grave, they hadn't done anything more dangerous than cross a military barracks fence to pretend they were gunmen—a place that was within the neighborhood's boundaries. That spring morning, Messi told Vallejos that he wouldn't return home until he found what he was looking for.

Vallejos still lives at his mother's house. He keeps some DVDs in a closet that he now pops into his TV's DVD player: Messi appears dressed up as a snail, and a woman's voice can be heard in the background narrating a story about a forest. Vallejos also appears in the video as a cricket. It's a school performance from their first days as students. They were playing insects in a forest with endangered animals—and their costumes were not rentals. Messi moves slowly, carrying a fabric-covered cardboard shell. The costume's seams reveal a dedicated family's long hours of hard work. Messi's childhood, the one his friends reminisce about and can be observed on this video, always happens in a world where a mother is waiting for him. The on-screen Messi is seen smiling in every take. His friend inserts another DVD and now La Pulga is twelve years old. He gets off a bus and says hi to the camera; then it cuts to an image of him mounting a mechanical bull. The fake animal bucks around and La Pulga topples onto a foam mat like a puppet. They are scenes from that end-of-year trip in Villa Carlos Paz. That trip was his farewell to the neighborhood. A few months later, he would be off to Barcelona and Diego Vallejos would start work at the tire factory. Then Vallejos became a father and, unknowingly, his life remained linked to the soccer player. His sister, Roxana Vallejos, is Matías Messi's girlfriend, the second of the three brothers. They have a child. It's the boy in Leo Messi's Black-Berry photo. He's the boy's godfather.

The friends now have a nephew in common.

"Leo seemed like he never did anything," says Vallejos. "But he did."

He had escaped his parents' house to see his grandmother's grave. Diego Vallejos didn't know this until they got back from the cemetery. And just like his friend Cintia Arellano, he wasn't aware that his friend had to inject himself with growth hormones.

La Pulga was secretive, and to his friends, he was a mystery.

Diego Vallejos preserves a letter Messi sent him when he was accepted into FC Barcelona. At the time, he lived in the Catalan La Masía. His writing is shaky.

"To a friend."

It is squared paper.

"Things are geting better each day in Soccer."

He doesn't care about spelling or grammar.

"At school I'm doing wors insted of better. But that's the least of my worries."

He couldn't care less about school.

"You have no idea how much I miss the street."

He's bored.

"I don't have any friends here and I spend my time at the movies."

He feels alone.

"Tell me about you. Do you have a girlfriend?"

He misses the neighborhood.

"I'm as lonely as a dog. Spanish girls are uglyer than XXX XX [two words are scratched out] I don't know what. Truth is I don't know what else to tell you so I leave you and send you a huge hug."

Writing tires him.

"PS1: Sorry for my writing and the paper."

He appreciates decent calligraphy.

"PS2: I love being an uncle."

Matías Messi has already had his first son with Vallejos's older sister.

The neighborhood was a refuge for Messi.

It was still so when he became a Barcelona star.

When the shaky writing turned into e-mails.

When the press pursued him.

"I'm sick of reporters and people," he wrote in 2005 to his agent, Fabián Soldini. "I'm always kind and always try to do my best. But reporters just cross the line. I know that when I get back [to Rosario] it won't be like that, and that makes me truly happy."

Nowadays, Leo Messi can't avoid moving around his city without being harassed by fans or a follower who demands goals for Argentina.

The last time he saw his neighborhood friends together was for his sister's fifteenth birthday. Messi had organized the party.

"Leo danced because we insisted," says Cintia Arellano. "He was never one to go to birthday parties. But on my birthday, he would stop by, even if just for a little bit."

His friend smiles as if she were receiving an award. Diego Vallejos feels a bit more distanced from Messi.

"Seeing each other was great," he tells me. "But I'm not used to so many luxuries."

Vallejos was the third person in the neighborhood who recommended I visit Messi's grandparents.

Christmas was only a few days away.

"Leo never visits," complains the grandfather, as do all grandparents.

The TV comedy is still running in the background.

The grandmother shakes her head.

The grandfather stares at the ground, then suddenly opens his eyes and raises his hand.

"And he's my grandson, darn it," he says, smacking the table with his fist.

"They're like that," murmurs the grandmother. "Kids go a little crazy. And now that he has money, it's even worse."

Her low voice simultaneously condemns and comprehends.

"Even though he doesn't come, as a grandmother, I still love him," she says. "But it's painful."

The photo of a victorious Messi still hangs on the grandparents' wall: He had been a champion with Argentina's national youth team, and since then, his image has remained frozen, an old promise in the lives of Argentines, grandparents, and the neighborhood. A champion grandson and a famous millionaire neighbor could mean the chance for change that everyone hopes for. That opportunity did not make it to Las Heras. Nor did it get to Pelé's Três Corações or Maradona's Villa Fiorito. It's the same naïveté of those who celebrate their country's actor winning an Oscar, or a cousin who just won the lottery. A star sparks mirages. Nowadays, those remaining in the neighborhood point you to Messi's grandparents' address.

# 13

In Zurich's Park Hyatt hotel lobby, Lionel Messi no longer pays attention to the jokes surrounding his bow tie. It's nighttime; he must get in the limo, listen to the jury's verdict, and get back to Barcelona. "I didn't expect to win today," he would declare a few hours later. The Kongresshaus, a building adjacent to the Limmat River, hosts the ceremony. Based on his goals and his play, a masterpiece of strength and speed, Messi's achievements are like a natural phenomenon. His mother, Celia Cuccittini, is wearing a black dress with a beaded neckline. Outside the hotel, as people talk, puffs of breath flow from their mouths. Celia Cuccittini's voice has the warmth of a mother who is telling you to put your coat on. Switzerland's cold mountain air can be felt on the street.

"This year there's no snow," observes his mom.

Mothers don't tend to concentrate on meteorological details when one of their children is about to receive an award. It's the Messi family's fourth visit to Switzerland to attend the same ceremony. The worst thing that can happen to him today is that he's voted the second- or third-best player in the world. Suddenly, an organized and quiet crowd surrounds him outside the hotel's entrance. The chauffeurs, bellboys, reporters, and players' families treat one another with that feigned courtesy imposed by great halls and gala clothing. For a moment, Messi wonders where he should place his hands and ends up sticking them in his pockets.

"Have you already bought an apartment in Zurich?" jokes a TV reporter.

He addresses Messi's father, who walks together with his wife.

"I haven't bought anything," responds Jorge Messi with distant charm. "But I've already seen some properties."

Polite laughter rings out in the background.

Messi's parents seem to share with their son the same way of experiencing the exotic as if it were normal. The Ballon d'Or atmosphere is a continuation of the days when La Pulga was first in line because he was short and his mother brought his trophies to school to show them to his teachers.

There's a big difference between charismatic brilliance to play soccer and muscular effectiveness to score goals. In 2011, Portuguese player Cristiano Ronaldo broke the historic scoring record in Real Madrid and La Liga with forty goals. He had already won a Ballon d'Or before this occasion. Messi surpassed his fellow countryman Alfredo Di Stéfano in the amount of consecutive wins with his team, and in 2010, he established himself as the highest scorer in

Barça's history within the Champions League. Cristiano Ronaldo wasn't featured on *Time*'s list of the 100 Most Influential People in the World. In 2011, Messi made the list and was mentioned right below U.S. president Barack Obama.

We like effective goals. We are hypnotized by someone's brilliance with a ball. Within the goal-scoring choreography, Messi is in charge of breaking the symmetry. One night at Camp Nou in 2011, after seeing Messi clear the ball over Arsenal's goalie's head in a Champions League match, Richard Williams, the *Guardian*'s sports analyst, described Messi as "a sweet soul that doles out damage." Vehemence is natural among children when they play, and they immediately identify it when seeking out playmates. If you add to that a huge desire to win, a civilized variant to a killer's instinct, the damage is irreversible.

"Taking care of Messi is easier than being Mick Jagger's bodyguard," says one of his bodyguards.

They call him "El Turco" (the Turk), a Rosario nightclub bouncer.

Rolling Stones fans are used to men like him who push them away from the glories of rock and roll.

"Children idolize Messi," explains the bodyguard. "But you can't push a kid away."

El Turco has taken care of Messi while he strolls through shopping malls. His father hired him because he knows his son doesn't only attract young fans. When the national team lost against Brazil in the South Africa World Cup qualifiers, Messi needed a security detail and El Turco wasn't around to protect him. That night, the defeat's frustration made one outraged fan leave a flashbang grenade at his home's door. The Las Heras neighborhood shook. In Barcelona, Messi can be seen alone, in shorts, getting money from an ATM. However, in Rosario, Messi is always a potential victim. Argentina's national team fans can begrudge missing goals with violence. Or his brilliance can be seen as a threat, resulting in a possible attack by a rival team. Messi was shaped in Newell's, and he knows the wrath those colors may awaken in Rosario Central fans. In 2011, around noon, while leaving a restaurant, Messi didn't even see the hand coming straight at his face. The scene was recorded.

Messi could've responded aggressively. When Eric Cantona wore Manchester United's jersey, he karate kicked a fan who insulted him from the stands. When Maradona played in Barça, he landed cleats-first on an Athletic Bilbao player's chest. Zidane lost his cool at the 2006 World Cup and head butted Italian defender Marco Materazzi. Messi confronted a Bolivian defender, without making it physical, during the first 2011 Copa América match. It was Messi's most violent scene within a record that is almost disappointing when it comes to wrath: There was note of an aimless gob of spit toward the defender, which the referee did not see. But one night at Camp Nou, Messi lifted his left hand and curled his fingers at Real Madrid's coach, José Mourinho. To the Spanish press, that was his biggest, most provocative gesture ever. He had just scored the goal that helped Barça win the 2011 Supercopa de España, and with his raised hand he was telling Mourinho that now he could talk. This year, Messi found his voice, and it went beyond scoring goals.

On that Rosario afternoon, someone diverted the hand that was aiming straight for Messi's face. The kamikaze's mother said her son was seventeen and he was sorry. Messi forgave him.

The same vehemence that surprises soccer commentators also pushes Messi to concentrate more on the game and ignore almost everything else. As a child, he'd practice after school, play on weekends, and, during his free time, compete with his brothers, father, uncle, and two of his three cousins: Maximiliano and Emanuel Biancucchi. Nowadays, they both earn a living doing the same thing. They all live in an insular world where the ball is the sun. Outside his team's boundaries, Messi hears a language that he prefers to not speak.

When trying things for the first time, player number 10 always chose his childhood teammates as his accomplices. Each time Messi organizes a barbecue, Leandro Benítez is always present. He was also a forward when La Pulga was a striker in Newell's minor leagues. He drinks *maté* with sugar, has long hair, and is nicknamed "El Negro." They started soccer at the same age. The same goes for sex. Messi arranged everything over the phone from Barcelona. It happened at his agent's Rosario apartment. Messi, Lucas Scaglia, and Benítez were fifteen. It was three of them with two girls. There were only two bedrooms.

"We met at a street corner and went," recalls Benítez. "Leo acted brave and didn't speak, but all three of us were scared."

Messi and Scaglia shared a room. Since then, the three friends have been inseparable. Nowadays, Messi shows his love when he scores a goal by bringing his hand with three extended fingers to his chest. Each finger is one of those accomplices from that first time.

Messi never denies that Rosario was where it all started. When committing to a relationship, he chose a girl whom he had liked as a child. To learn how to drive, he didn't choose a desolate Catalan road; he did it with a green Ford Escort in Rosario's Urquiza Park. Nowadays, Leandro Benítez has the same agent who led them to their first debut as children; he plays as a Chacarita Juniors defender in Buenos Aires and says that La Pulga always e-mails him. Sometimes he tells Benítez to stop by a sports store to pick up clothes he's left under his name.

"I've never asked him for anything," says Benítez. "But we know what kind of person he is."

His lack of goals with Argentina's national team makes people question his *Argentineness*. He insists on being Argentine and is still loyal to his origins, even if they threaten him. One dawn in 2007, after flying to his country to recover from an injury, the soccer player went to a bar close to his house with his two brothers. One man stood up and began to insult him. Once again, he was being assailed for defending the Newell's jersey. Days later, Messi appeared in a newspaper section that had nothing to do with sports: The crime blotter stated that the Barça player had gotten into a fistfight and was being sued for breaking chairs and a window and for leaving without closing out his bill. For the first time, Messi had to face criminal charges. His brothers, obviously, became secondary characters in the breaking story.

"Leo is the calmest guy I've ever met in my life," his

bodyguard assures me. "The only times I've had problems with him were when his brother was around."

Apart from being his bodyguard, El Turco sometimes runs into Messi at the Rosario nightclubs where he works. One night at La Misión del Marinero, he saw a man defiantly pointing a finger at Messi.

"It wasn't serious," said El Turco. "But then his brother jumped in and started a fight."

"And what did Messi do?"

"He got scared and we had to get him out of there."

Matías Messi is the second of the three brothers and the only one who still lives in Rosario. El Turco says that Matías has put him in uncomfortable positions as a nightclub bouncer on more than one occasion.

"Another night he started screaming. He was out of control and we had to calm him down," says the bodyguard. "He said that they didn't want to take him to Spain because he was a disgrace to his family."

Tonight, on this evening in Zurich, Matías Messi is absent. The family is incomplete at the Ballon d'Or award ceremony. In addition to his parents and sister, Messi has invited an uncle, an aunt, and a cousin. According to protocol, the limo will take them to the venue where the best player in the world will be revealed. The night that man insulted him for defending the colors of his childhood team, and then accused him of breaking a window and hitting a couple at the bar, Lionel Messi was one of the people who held his brother back. However, he remained silent in front of the police and the press. The younger brother let the blame fall only on him.

# 14

Every time Leo Messi lands in Argentina, his second brother is there to greet him. Those who are close to him know that he's the one who makes Messi laugh. His second brother doesn't carry the same responsibilities as the eldest, who is his chef and security director. The second brother isn't spoiled by his family, as his sister is, who wants to be like Leo Messi but in the theater. When La Pulga played the 2005 U-20 World Cup in the Netherlands, he asked his agent to pay for one more first-class plane ticket: Matías Messi was his accomplice. He wanted to be with him when he traveled to Buenos Aires before leaving for Germany and, from there, the World Cup. Player number 10 booked a double room at the hotel so he could be with his brother. Matías Messi had asked him to be his first son's godfather. The second brother has Messi's image tattooed on his left arm. Each time he finishes an important game, Messi gives his jersey and cleats to his brother. At his Rosario home, the second Messi brother has created a family museum filled with soccer balls, jerseys, shoes, and photos. He's a fraternal fetishist.

He's usually not mentioned in the press, so his face is unknown by the public. Tonight, he is wearing a pair of shorts and smells of cologne. He is standing in the exact spot where the police detained him two years earlier for carrying a gun in his waistband: the corner of Uriburu Avenue and Primavero de Mayo Street, in Las Heras, half a block away from his grandparents' house. The .32 caliber gun was loaded with five bullets. The news wouldn't have been as important if his last name hadn't been Messi. The best player in the world is required to lead an exemplary life, and Matías keeps frequenting his neighborhood's poorer areas. He has seven criminal charges, two linked to assaulting women. The others are for street fights and traffic accidents. They call him El Rebelde (the Rebel) at home. In a family where everyone is a soccer fan and Newell's follower, Matías Messi is the only brother who decided not to be a soccer player. He also became a Rosario Central fan.

Nowadays, Matías Messi kills time on a Las Heras street corner. He earns his keep by helping his father manage his brother's fortune and a bar La Pulga bought next to the Paraná River. Each time he visits, player number 10 tries to be with his coconspirator. In essence, returning to Rosario is to Messi what coming home equals to any immigrant: reconnecting with the past's happiness and problems. However, Matías Messi has not just created a museum with his brother's items; he guards a world that

La Pulga no longer frequents. And now he keeps an eye on me.

"What are you looking for?" he says.

He crosses his arms and raises his chin. He's wearing silver earrings with fake diamond studs.

"I thought you were robbing my grandparents."

"I just spoke with them and they didn't say anything about someone robbing them," I say.

"They don't even notice," says the grandson. "But every day someone comes along and gives them fake bills."

The house's windows, which serve as the bakery windows, are open, and through them you can see his grandfather watching TV while leaning over a plate of food. It smells like soup, and the room is dark. It's where La Pulga would've been had he not made it to the club that paid for his hormone treatment, which allowed him to grow. When Messi left for Spain for the first time, Matías accompanied him together with the whole family. They were all going to live there.

"My sister and I wanted to come back," he says. "My brothers decided to stay. They're more like my old man: Things matter to them a bit more than they do to me."

Matías Messi came back from Barcelona four months later. Now he believes that was a mistake.

"When I came back and my brother stayed there, I felt I had abandoned him."

Dogs bark in the background.

"I never thought Leo would get so far in so little time," he admits. "Sometimes my mom and I say we regret having left him."

The brother's voice cracks.

"He's got such a good heart," says Fabián Soldini about Matías. "Leo adores him because of his situation."

Messi's ex-agent lived within the family circle during their first five years in Barcelona.

The situation that Soldini is referring to is what some people talk about in Rosario.

They say Matías Messi is a drug addict.

Public figures tend to have difficult siblings. One of Bill Clinton's brothers was a convicted felon under drug charges, and he received a presidential acquittal. Former president of Mexico Carlos Salinas de Gortari's brother was accused of homicide and was incarcerated in the prison his brother had constructed during his term in office. One of Elton John's brothers lives in a humble shed. Family trees are packed with scandals, but they never overshadow the family star's popularity.

Leo Messi never abandoned his brother.

"I so feel like seeing my little nephew," says an e-mail Messi sent Soldini three years after he moved to Barcelona. "They are such characters at this age that I love to be with them."

At the time, his nephew, Tomás Messi, was two years old.

To La Pulga, the trip to Spain meant more than the start of a professional career and payment for his growth treatment.

"There were several dreams surrounding this move," says Jorge Messi to me over the phone. "The idea was to help Lionel and also better our lives."

The whole family flew to Barcelona on February 1, 2001. At the airport, says Soldini, Messi's parents approached him.

"We have to thank you for the rest of our lives," he recalls them saying. "Not because of Leo, but because of Matías, for getting him out of there."

During the uncertain start at Barça, Lionel Messi challenged his entire family to believe in him. The second brother found it hard to think he would find something better than what he had left behind in Rosario. He was going out with Roxana Vallejos, a girl from the neighborhood who now is his wife and mother to Messi's godson. Diego Vallejos, her brother and the soccer player's friend, glances to the side when I mention his brother-in-law.

"I hardly speak to Matías," says Vallejos. "I prefer not to talk about him. I might say something that will bother the family."

When the police detained him for carrying a firearm, Matías Messi's name was on the front page of the newspaper *La Capital de Rosario*. The following day, his father called the journalist who had written the article, and they met at a bar.

"The father was distressed," says Hernán Lascano to me one afternoon in Rosario.

He was the first one to make headlines and splash the family's intimate life all over the city's most important newspaper. Lascano expected Messi's father to be furious. Yet Jorge Messi only wanted to ask him for a favor: to please contact him before publishing anything else, so he could explain his son's problem. He didn't want to deny anything but rather make sure that Lascano had the story straight.

That night, in Las Heras, Matías Messi enters into further detail.

"I was crazy," he tells me. "You go a little crazy because you see him everywhere."

Two men appear to his left. One has gray hair and the other has a shaved head. He looks like a skinhead.

"To this day I can't get used to it," he continues, as if we were alone. "Leo's on TV and I can't keep walking. I stop and watch; I watch him a thousand times."

"Did you play soccer? Why did you give it up?"

"Because I was lazy," says Matías.

The gray-haired guy and skinhead observe him from a distance.

"If Leo had to play at nine thirty, he was the first to get up," he says. "He likes what he does."

Before his brothers even noticed, La Pulga set foot on a soccer field and started to capture the attention of his parents, the neighborhood, and Rosario. Facing a brother whose image is tattooed on his arm and whom he'd like to stop seeing everywhere but can't, Matías Messi was left in an uncomfortable position, which any superstitious brother could imagine. One winter night, he went to a Champions League soccer match where Barça was playing against Chelsea. That night, in London's Stamford Bridge stadium, they injured his brother.

"I sat in a section I never usually sit at," he tells me. "So I said: 'It's my fault.'"

Matías Messi thinks he brings his brother bad luck. He always sits to Rodrigo's right.

"Always to the right," he repeats.

That night, he had sat to Rodrigo's left. After that game, La Pulga flew to Rosario with his dad and brothers to recover from his injury. Months later, someone insulted him at a bar and, after a fight, Lionel Messi was the only one held responsible with a criminal complaint. Matías was there that night too, convinced his presence brings bad luck. Two years later he'd explain it to the cops who detained him for carrying a gun; it would go in their report: "Matías Messi blames himself for his brother's bad soccer performance and his father's illness." At the time, his dad was undergoing medical exams to see if he had cancer. His middle son felt guilty.

Tonight, Matías Messi stops pitying himself and introduces me to the two men who approached us. They are two neighbors.

I ask the reason he's never featured on TV or in photos.

"I don't like it," he tells me. "It's dangerous."

"Why is it dangerous?"

"In case they kidnap you," he replies, like someone repeating something that should be obvious. "Anything can happen to you here."

Months after this chat with him on a Las Heras street corner, someone would open fire at the front of his house. They unloaded six shots. Matías Messi would declare to the press that he did not know the reason. At the time, his brother was preparing to play a classic and decisive game against Real Madrid, and the press speculated that the gunshots had been an attempt to distract the Argentine player. The other Messi, who feels responsible for his brother's few moments of bad luck, will have yet another chance to feel guilty.

# 15

The last time Messi wore a suit in public was during a trip with Barça to Stuttgart, in 2010, and when he exited the plane, his shoelaces were untied. For photographers searching for any minute detail, it was a happy melody in the silent movie that makes up his private life in Europe. But on this night, on Zurich's freezing sidewalks, when the TV cameras and lenses focus on him, Messi's shoelaces are tied and his bow tie is intact while entering the Kongresshaus where the Ballon d'Or will be announced. Two years earlier, this event's red carpet was around thirty-two feet long. Now it's as long as an Olympic-size swimming pool. When Johan Cruyff received the same award, the media coverage resulted in his landing on the cover of *France Football* magazine, which back then was the only event organizer (today FIFA cosponsors the event). The celebrated soccer players take their time on the red carpet, and the publicists use those seconds on TV to show off the new soccer heroes' gala wear. Nowadays, any of Messi's public events, or even the involuntary act of showing up with untied shoelaces, can turn into a disproportionate publicity event.

Messi is a modern phenomenon. Excitement promotes intrigue, and his small stature only serves to amplify his soccer status. On the carpet that leads the three Ballon d'Or nominees inside, the candidates—Messi, Hernández, and Iniesta—seem out of place: If they were boxers, they'd be welterweights. Size doesn't matter in the world's best soccer club. Today's most celebrated soccer triangle is not equilateral, it's telepathic. If they were Olympic athletes, Hernández, Iniesta, and Messi could be part of a synchronized swimming team. Messi's game, quasi-sterile of goals on his national team, is fertile when accompanied by these two in Barça. The writer Fernando Iwasaki once said that Maradona scored the most beautiful goal in history because he was unable to pass the ball to Jorge Valdano, and that was the best metaphor for team play.

Maradona never registered his trademark second goal against England in the Mexico World Cup, and now he doesn't even earn a cent every time it is replayed on TV. However, Valdano did register his idea "pensar corriendo" (to think while running), and now he is a consultant thanks to his elite competition experience. Maradona was the best at one thing only: playing ball (although he also produced famous catchphrases); Valdano is good at everything he does. Messi, regarding his future, only mentions he'll move back to Rosario—the same city where his father manages his fortune from the eleventh floor of a glass building. Like

Maradona, Messi does not apply his brilliance to anything else other than playing soccer. However, like Valdano, at least in Barça and with his family, number 10 ensures his future by being a team player.

Tonight, under the lights of Zurich's Kongresshaus, Messi makes a gesture that does not go well with his tuxedo: He sticks out his tongue, which touches his chin. Once again, he's here to mock the statistics: Pelé was the king of soccer for twelve years; Cruyff seized the crown in a cloud of cigarette smoke for five years; Maradona reigned for ten years; Ronaldo used his potential, albeit irregularly, to lead for a decade; Ronaldinho smiled for only four seasons; and Zidane was a brief monarch, belated in his success but elegant into the twilight of his career. Messi gets up from his seat with the languid movements of one who is not hurried and has a long ways to go. The TV cameras zoom in on his face. Some awards at times turn the soccer experts white with anger; awards that some years are presented only because they have to be, such as those received by Michael Owen, Pavel Nedvěd, or Fabio Cannavaro—at times extraordinary soccer players, but irregular in their performance and far from brilliant. These fleeting stars only highlight the regularity of authentic geniuses, such as Pelé, Cruyff, Maradona, Zidane, and Messi, who at this hour of the night approaches the podium, from which he will give thanks for the Ballon d'Or. Instead of moving the microphone to his mouth, Messi leans over it. Later, he'd say he did it that way because his legs were shaking. In a few months he'd be seen chin up and frowning, trying to lead Argentina's national team in the Copa América, and later crying when eliminated in the quarterfinals. Months earlier, he was facing a microphone and TV cameras to say a few words in a Camp Nou full of fans who had gone there to celebrate Barça's Champions League victory. At last, one hundred thousand members of the audience would get to hear his words.

"In truth," Messi said, "I have nothing to say."

But on this 2011 night, he thanks his teammates who helped him get there; he wants to share this award with them, his family, the Barça fans, and all the Argentines. He kisses the Ballon d'Or in Zurich, and his shoelaces remain tied. His smooth Italian leather footwear have the look and feel of gloves. He still drags his heels when he walks, with outward-turned feet, as if he is wearing the blue flip-flops he puts on after training with Barça, before heading to lunch—those flip-flops that give him that somewhat lethargic and sleepy Sunday feel of someone who doesn't mind being late. Or who is going to sleep.

Messi is the inevitable standard his siblings, friends, and neighbors have to measure themselves against. We humans usually need a point of reference to see how far we grow, and Messi, as the neighborhood kid with growing problems, has become a hopeful mirage. When he thanked the doctor who designed his growth treatment on TV, the endocrinologist's practice began to receive dozens of calls from patients who wanted to increase their height. His doctor, Diego Schwarzstein, had to explain that he could only treat those who suffered from a growth hormone deficiency and that they were simply genetically short.

"If it were possible to make anyone grow, I'd play in the

NBA," said the doctor one afternoon when he welcomed me to his Rosario practice.

The man who helped Messi grow is a little over five feet six inches tall—less than half an inch taller than his most famous patient.

"What would have happened if Messi hadn't injected himself with hormones?"

"He'd be a four feet eleven inches tall."

Today Messi is seven inches taller than that.

He has reached higher levels than any other soccer player his age. Before turning twenty-five, he has established himself as the top scorer in Barça history; has won the Club World Cup twice with his team; has become the face of an energy drink in China, a microwave manufacturer in Japan, and a fast-food chain in the United Arab Emirates—countries in which decades earlier the business of soccer was still regarded as an exotic curiosity. For the third consecutive year, he has been chosen in Zurich as the best soccer player in the world. It would be his last international award before Guardiola decided to step down as Barça manager. In January 2012, dressed in a purple Dolce & Gabanna velvet suit, Messi joined the elite ranks of Johan Cruyff, Michel Platini, and Marco van Basten, the only other players with three Ballons d'Or. Messi is the youngest player to have ever achieved this triple honor, and after Platini, he is only the second to have received it consecutively, as well as the only Latin American on the list. His genius on the field, so precocious and frequently displayed, makes fans worry excessively about his future beyond soccer. In Yokohama Stadium, after Messi was selected as the best player of the Club World Cup, a Japanese television reporter approached him to ask about his life after soccer.

"I don't know," Messi told him. "There's a lot of time left before that happens."

His possible retirement from the sport causes anxiety. Messi has before him a decade to keep scoring goals.

Schwarzstein smiles as if remembering some mischief.

"The most moving part of the treatment," he says, "is that the kids who receive it see their friends growing, but they grow even faster; they reach them and pass them. That makes them very happy. It's what happened to Leo."

The type of dwarfism that Messi suffered occurs in one of every twenty thousand births. The treatment against bone age delay lets patients grow quickly when they begin to inject themselves with synthetic hormones. Dr. Schwarzstein stresses that suddenly growing is not only a physical experience but also an emotional one. At an age where we still believe in cartoons, suddenly growing artificially is like making a dream come true. La Pulga had the starring role in that story.

## ACKNOWLEDGMENTS

---------------------------------

To Julio Villanueva Chang, friend and severe editor of each of these pages.

To Toño Angulo Daneri, Diego Salazar, Jordi Carrión, and Roberto Herrscher Rovira, for their careful reading.

To Cécile Carrez, for her research help and daily support; to Álvaro Sialer, for his fact-checking zeal; to Graciela Mangusi, for her legal advice, and to Lizzy Cantú, for her hours dedicated to rereading.

This book would not have been possible without the following people's confidence: Miguel Aguilar, Claudio López de Lamadrid, and Gaby Wiener, my generous assistant. I also thank María Lynch for her patient support.

To Ramón Besa and Ezequiel Fernández Moores, constant and timely advisers. To Martín Caparrós, who responded to my e-mails with questions disguised as answers, and to Juan Villoro, for sparing some time to talk about soccer even though he was running late for a dinner.

To my sports press friends who shared their time and their archives: Ramiro Martín, Marcelo Sottile, Felip Vivanco, Cristina Cubero, Toni Frieros, David Bernabeu, and Luca Caioli. Thanks as well to Carles Geli, Mauro Federico, Maximiliano Tomas, Felipe Trueba, and Gabriela Calotti.

To my sister, Lorena Faccio, and to Norma and Óscar Corubolo, for arriving at the right time in the story.

Thanks to my aunt Marta Faccio, Giulia Luisetti, Alfonso Gastiaburo, and Isabel Rozey and Josep Maria Camps, for letting your homes be mine as well.

To Juan Pedro Chuet-Missé, for the accumulated years of unconditional support.

To all the people in Buenos Aires, Rosario, and Barcelona who trusted me and agreed to tell their stories.

To Lionel Messi and his family, for the time given during the giddiest years of their lives.